The True Ghost Stori

Volume 6

50 Fantastic and Frightening Tales

Elisabeth Busch

Web: ghosts.org
Email: stories@ghosts.org

Also by Elisabeth Busch:

The True Ghost Stories Archive: Volume 1 (2019)
The True Ghost Stories Archive: Volume 2 (2019)
The True Ghost Stories Archive: Volume 3 (2019)
The True Ghost Stories Archive: Volume 4 (2019)
The True Ghost Stories Archive: Volume 5 (2020)
The True Ghost Stories Archive: Volume 7 (2020)
The True Ghost Stories Archive: Volume 8 (2020)
The True Ghost Stories Archive: Volume 9 (2020)
The True Ghost Stories Archive: Volume 10 (2020)
The True Ghost Stories Archive: Volume 11 (2020)
The True Ghost Stories Archive: Volume 12 (2020)
The True Ghost Stories Archive: Volume 13 (2020)
Tiny but True Ghost Tales (2019)
A Survey of North American Spooklights: Eyewitness Accounts and Information on 20 Anomalous Lights (2020)
The Real Top 1000 Baby Names: Combined spellings, real meanings, current trends, & newly rising names (2018)

Table of Contents

Sign up for the True Ghost Stories Mailing List at

ghosts.org

to receive weekly true stories, plus a free ebook of

Tiny but True Ghost Tales: 30 Spooky Supernatural Stories

Send stories, questions, and comments to

obiwan@ghosts.org.

Introduction

From 1993 until sometime in the mid-2000s, I actively maintained a true ghost story FTP site, mailing list, and web archive on my personal domain, ghosts.org. Initially, the stories came from the early years of the alt.folklore.ghost-stories USENET newsgroup, but as time marched on most of them were submitted directly to me through email, my website, or the mailing list. At its height, the True Ghost Stories Archive held over 2000 stories, culled from many more thousands of submissions.

During those years, I was fancifully known to readers of my website and mailing list as Obiwan. I had picked up this moniker during the early 1990s in college, when our user names were limited to eight characters or less. My last name+first initial had the nerve to add up to nine characters, which precluded its use on our ancient computer network and forced me to get creative. This is why you will see some stories in these volumes beginning with "Dear Obiwan" or similar things.

The oldest entry in the archives was sent to me in 1994. However, the stories span a much greater historical timeline than that, with the earliest first person remembrance being from the 1920s and the latest from around 2008. Some of the storytellers were elderly in the 1990s when they wrote to me and, unfortunately, have probably passed on. It seems fitting that their memories are preserved here, and we are lucky to have them.

I debated for some time over how to format the entries. I considered several options, ranging from not touching the original text at all to completely rewording the stories to maximize anonymity. I also dithered over what to do with the opening and closing text of the entries, as they often begin with personal salutations and end with appeals for discussion or help. In the end, I left everything largely intact, electing only to fix egregious grammar/spelling mistakes, split paragraphs for readability, or clarify a statement here and there. I did, however, make an effort to obscure specific personal and place names where privacy might be an issue. I also deleted the original message headers and signatures as I felt many of them contained too much personal information. The names and locations of publicly accessible places have been left intact.

My main intent in publishing these stories is to preserve them. Some of the older USENET posts are now unfindable, probably deleted from news servers before they could be archived, and even a few of the entries in my own archives became corrupted or went missing over time due to database issues. I have chosen for these volumes the most reader-friendly stories in the archives, while the remainder are being republished on ghosts.org. I hope you enjoy reading them as much as I've enjoyed collecting them over the years.

Elisabeth Busch
January 2020

Little Boy Ghost

Date posted: June 1998

Okay, I lied. I'm going to post one actual ghost story before going to sleep. This is wicked long, but chock full of stuff. Enjoy.

My mom and dad bought our house in 1973, a year before I was born. It was a fixer-upper, to say the least, a 250 year old Cape style on the backroads of Maine. One family had been living in the house for generations, until it was finally put on the market. There are rumors that the house was used to run slaves long ago, that a man related to the family who owned the house had shot himself in the back field, and that the land around the house is the burial ground of a once-local tribe of Native Americans. It is an old house, and bears the scars of different inhabitants and renovation.

Anyway, my mom and dad were working to fix the house up so they could live in it. They had to rebuild the fireplaces (there are three, all on a central flue), build steps to the cellar as there was nothing more than a hole in the floor and a ladder, and do other work with the windows and door casings.

My mother tells me that often when she was working alone in the house, things would turn up missing. One time in particular she remembers using a screwdriver to scrape the dirt from between the floorboards. She put it down to go get something to drink, and when she came back it was gone. My mom is a believer in the paranormal, so she put her hands on her hips and said, "Now, I'm trying to fix this house up, and if you keep hiding things on me it isn't going to help." She left the room for a few minutes and relaxed, and when she returned the screwdriver was back where she left it.

My dad, who is a great skeptic and doesn't believe in any sort of paranormal things, was working in the cellar one afternoon. He had told my brother, who was three at the time, not to go near the cellar hole as there were no stairs yet and he would fall in. My dad was coming up the ladder from the cellar and his head had just come up to the same level of the floor when he saw a pair of child's feet clad in shoes and shorts run by the hole. Thinking it was my brother, my dad yelled out, "Billy! I thought I told you to stay away from this hole!" My mom heard him and came inside to ask him what was wrong. When my dad told her what he saw, she said that Billy was outside with her, playing in the yard.

My dad saw this child a second time. One night he fell asleep on the couch while watching television, and woke up to that creepy wee-hours static. He looked up and saw a fair-haired little boy in striped pajamas sitting cross-legged in front of the TV. Again, thinking it to be my brother, who was young and fair-haired as well, he said, "Billy, go to bed." The child ignored him, and he repeated himself. This time the child turned his head towards my dad, and it wasn't my brother. With that, the child disappeared.

My mother also saw the child. One night she awoke and saw the little boy, in striped pajamas, standing in front of the window next to her bed, looking out. She thought it was Billy (poor kid got blamed for everything) and said, "Billy, go to bed." The child ignored her, she repeated herself, and you guessed it—the kid turned to her and wasn't Billy. She then describes it disappearing as if it were collapsing into itself, like "water going down a drain" she described it, and then it was gone. She woke up my dad and was pretty shaken up by the whole ordeal.

That's all for tonight, but I have plenty more for future posts. A funny note to end on... my brother once spent the day chasing our chickens around the pen and generally terrorizing them (I forgot to mention I grew up on a farm). He had a vivid nightmare that night that a giant chicken was standing on the footboard of his bed, pecking him. He swears that he was awake and that the giant chicken was real. His screaming woke up my mom and she hurried to his room, and the chicken disappeared.

So what are the morals to my stories? Don't run in the house, we had the idea long before Poltergeist the movie, and be kind to animals. Goodnight!

Children Calling

Date received: February 2002

Hey All!

This is my first time posting a story on this site, or any site for that matter, but I hope you can appreciate what I have to say.

I've always been interested in the paranormal even though I am a strong Christian, but only had little experiences until I was in the eighth grade. Here is my first big experience. I don't know why it happened or where they came from, but it scared the hell out of me.

It was about 11:00 on a school night, and I was watching TV in my room when my mom called my name and told me to go let my dogs in. I bounded down the stairs to the back door and swung it open. I immediately called my dogs' names. The younger dog, Bo, came flying down the "bridge." This was part of my back deck that connected the deck to the backyard, leading over a huge ditch that was dug so you could go under my pool. Bo flew past me into the house. The other dog, Alex, who was much older, 13 at the time, would not come.

It was really cold and windy that night, although the wind wasn't making any noise. If you stood in the doorway, in the backyard directly to your left was a huge oak tree. I started to get an eerie feeling, and then I heard something that sounded like children's voices emanating from behind the oak tree. The voices were calling something that sounded like my name.

I started to freak and frantically called Alex's name. He finally came up the bridge but stopped at the end where the stairs were. Since he was so old he had arthritis in his hips and couldn't get down the stairs well without assistance. Again, I heard the voices calling. They grew louder and it soon sounded as if there were double the children calling my name. I was starting to cry in panic and fear. Fear of those voices, and fear that somehow they may harm my dog. Still, there was no way I was going out there to get him.

They grew louder and giggled as they spoke. I answered them with a defiant "no" under my breath and slammed the door without getting the dog in. I flew up the stairs to my parents' bedroom and firmly reported, "That stupid dog won't come in. You get him." With that, I went in my room, closed my blinds, jumped into bed, and tried to sleep.

I know that these voices weren't "live" children because at the time it happened it was extremely late and a school night, and the voices sounded so young. Also, the houses surrounding mine didn't house children, and if they did, what would they be doing behind my oak tree at eleven o' clock on a school night? They couldn't get over my fence anyway.

This event was just the beginning of my experiences. Later, when I retold the story to my mother, she seemed disturbed but believed me. If you want, I have many more stories and I will send them if you'd like.

Bubble People

Date posted: October 1995

Hi there. I've been lurking for some time now, posting an occasional comment or question. But many of the stories shared have resurfaced a few memories of the house in which I grew up. I thought it would be fun to share them and attempt to give back to the group that has given me much to think about. This may be long, so you may choose to print it out and read it at your leisure.

First of all, let me tell you a bit about the house itself. It's located in "The Avenues" of Salt Lake City, Utah and was built in the 1800s. To add to the ambiance, there is one of the largest graveyards in the nation right across the street. It was fun growing up across the street from a graveyard, especially around Halloween, but I don't think it really had anything to do with the strange occurrences in the house.

There would be the usual sounds of an old house—the creaks and groans and occasional footsteps on the stairs. The basement was very eerie, as most are. There was one room in the basement, however, that was the most disturbing. No one ever went in there unless it was very necessary. And no one stayed in there longer than they had to. My brother and I would swear we saw eyes watching us from that dark room sometimes.

My family moved into the house when my older brother was three or four years old, and I was born into the house not long after. The "experiences" tended to center around my brother and seemed to sympathize with him and his having to deal with a bratty younger sister always playing with his toys and tagging around after him.

My brother had many dreams in which it seemed the house was trying to communicate with him. He told me of many dreams in which the house "told" him about previous residents, one dream being of small children writing on the living room walls, and an adult, maybe a parent, yelling at the children. Not long after, my parents decided to do some remodeling in that room and had a "wall stripping" party. Friends and relatives spent days at our house scraping off what seemed like hundreds of layers of paint and wallpaper. Sure enough, one of the layers had writings in what looked like crayon and markers of things like "1 + 1 = 2." My brother and I told my parents about the dream he had had, but they brushed it off as coincidence or a child's imagination. My father has since passed away, and my mother is still an adamant disbeliever in the supernatural.

The upstairs consisted of a hallway with my brother's room on one end and my room on the other. One night my brother and I were in our separate rooms. My brother had about seven or eight posters hanging up in his room at the time, some on the ceiling and some on the walls. I was lying in my bed reading when I heard these posters falling. Wondering what was going on, I went into my brother's room and found him sitting up in his bed with a look of astonishment. Every single poster had fallen at the exact same time! By this time we had become used to unusual occurrences and accepted it as the mischievous ghost having some fun.

Another occurrence happened when I was nine or ten years old. A friend and I were playing "school" in a room that had been made into a study. I was sitting on the floor, busy writing on a chalkboard, and my friend was making up assignments from a book. My parents had been doing some kind of construction in the house, and this room was often used to store excess junk. So it was not unusual to have a small piece of wood lying on the floor next to my leg. This particular piece of wood had a pointed end, which started to poke my leg. I was concentrating on my work on the chalkboard and didn't pay much attention to it at first. I thought it was my friend inadvertently pushing it as she moved about. Then it became annoying, so I turned to tell my friend to stop poking me with this piece of wood when I noticed that she was clear across the room, nowhere near me or the wood!

Similar things would happen, just small, friendly reminders that something else besides us inhabited the house. Our parents never seemed to be bothered by anything, though, and always told us that it was just our imagination.

The occurrences weren't always taken so lightly, however. I do remember seeing "the bubble people" at night, which were like small, round, colorful lights that hovered around my room, usually seen from the corner of my eye. They had faces that showed expressions of giddiness, happiness, and playfulness. I feared them at first, and would go running downstairs to my mother, who would escort me back up to bed, telling me it was just my imagination.

One night, however, I was lying in bed trying to fall asleep when I saw a very large "bubble person" by my bedroom door. It was a very dark night, and he was showing up quite vividly, just hovering there. And, unlike most of the bubble people I saw, he didn't disappear when I stared at him. He was also not as happy-looking as the other apparitions. In fact, he had a kind of malevolent look to his expression. And he was multi-colored rather than one solid color, which was again unusual for the bubble people.

After staring at each other for a while, I decided to get a closer look. Gathering up all my courage, I crawled out of bed and slowly approached it, never taking my eyes off its floating face. Then I realized, hey, this is probably just my brother and cousin (who was staying with us at the time) trying to scare me! In fact, this did look kind of like a paper mache mask my brother made in school. With a sigh of relief, I swatted at the mask to show the pranksters that I caught their little joke. To my amazement, my hand went right through the apparition, and it was still there, right in front of me. Terrified, I ran downstairs to mom, screaming and crying. Once again, she told me it was just my imagination, and stayed with me until I finally fell asleep.

Many years later I would discover that my brother also saw the bubble people, and we finally decided that it might not be our imaginations after all.

We had a cream-colored, plush-upholstered sectional couch in the living room that, similar to velvet, would appear to darken and lighten when you brushed the fabric one way or the other. One day my brother and I were watching TV when I noticed a perfect skull imprinted in the back of the couch. I thought maybe my brother might have "drawn" it there with his fingers earlier, and told him it was pretty cool-looking. He looked at the couch and said he hadn't drawn it. Then he pointed out the rest of the skeleton—the torso, legs, and arms. All perfectly proportional as if someone very artistic had made it. My parents had been out of town during this time, and no one else had been in the house. So who could have drawn this skeleton into the couch? It spooked me out, so I brushed it away, never to see it resurface again.

My great aunt travelled around the world and brought wonderful souvenirs for us. One of the presents she brought for me was a crocheted doll from I think it was Brazil. It was kind of spooky-looking to me, and I never really liked it, but it was a present from a beloved relative and it was mine.

On several occasions I would find the doll in my brother's room. I would always be infuriated with him for taking my doll, and would snatch it back to put in its proper place, which was on the downstairs bookcases, since I couldn't sleep with it in my room. Inevitably, it would find its way back to my brother's room. When I would yell at him for taking my doll, he would claim that he thought I had put it there. He didn't like this doll much, either.

Then we moved out of the house to a condo on the Upper East Side. I never remember packing the doll, and neither did my brother or mother. As a matter of fact, we had all seemed to forget about the doll. But a few days after moving into the new home, it was there in my brother's room.

When my brother moved out, he left the doll on the bookshelf where I liked to keep it. Then one day it wasn't on the bookshelf anymore. And sure enough, when we went to visit my brother in his new apartment, there was the doll. I mentioned the doll to my brother, telling him that he should have told me he was taking it. But he insisted that he didn't take it. A few years later, he moved from that apartment to another, and left the doll in the old apartment for the new tenants. He didn't like the doll and didn't want it. Yet again it followed him to his new residence, showing up in one of the packed boxes. He finally accepted that he would never be able to get rid of it and simply packed it up whenever he moved.

Today my brother lives in the old house with his wife and son. Strange occurrences rarely happen anymore, he says. Every once in a while he will not be able to turn off his computer. He will turn it off and it will come back on. The only way he can keep it from turning itself back on is by unplugging it. And this is with relatively new wiring in the house. And his three year old son sometimes talks to someone no one else can see. Perhaps just an imaginary friend, perhaps not. But my brother has vowed never to tell him that what he sees is "just his imagination."

Thanks for listening. Comments/questions welcomed.

Closet Monster

Date received: September 1998

When I was about twelve years old my father bought me a Ouija board, the typical one found in toy stores. I didn't learn about use of the board until years later, so of course I didn't follow the rules. I used it alone, didn't say goodbye at the end, and left the hand piece facing down on the board when I put it away. I kept this board in the walk-in closet in our computer room that was right next to the computer.

One day, I was home alone playing a game on our computer sitting next to the closet. The door to the closet, fortunately, was closed. While I was on the computer I heard a growl in the closet and something began to bang on the door as if trying to get out. I could actually see the door banging around. Now, there was not an earthquake that day and we really don't get them. I was the only one in the house, and my dog was outside. I didn't bother to look in the closet—I was too busy sprinting out of there as fast as I could. I ran outside and down the street and waited until my mother came home.

I didn't talk about this incident until I was 18. I also didn't use that board. By that time I had seen the movie Witchboard and was convinced I had somehow done something wrong. I had a friend at that time who knew quite a bit about the supernatural. I told him about it and he took the board away. I don't know what he did with it.

A few years ago in my early 20s I was talking to my youngest sister. There are four of us; I am the oldest and she is ten years younger than I am. Somehow, the computer room was brought up. I said I hated going in there because it was scary. Her eyes got big and she told me how much she was scared of it too, like something was in there. I told her about my incident years ago. I was somewhat relieved that someone else was afraid of that room and it wasn't just my overactive imagination.

There is about a 0% possibility of my parents' house being haunted. The house was built in the 1970s and only one other family has lived in it. I knew that family and no one has died there. Before houses were built there, the entire area was used as farmland. So there can't be any spirits there from that. The only thing I can think of is something came through the board. I just wonder if it's still there. My sister and I still have feelings in that room.

China Cabinet

Date posted: March 1999

Well, this is a brand new house, only two years old, in a new subdivision.

The first odd thing that happened was about a year or more ago. This house has an open floor plan, meaning the living, dining, and kitchen are all one big room. The master bedroom is on one side of the house, and the other two bedrooms are on the other. So, to get from the master to the other room, you walk a straight line across the great room.

Anyway, I was cleaning house, and had gone through some magazines and then put them on the floor in an orderly pile next to the garbage can. I continued cleaning back and forth across the house. After spending about ten minutes in the master bedroom, I left the room to cross the house. There, right in my path, was the top magazine that I'd left on the floor in the kitchen. Somehow, it had relocated itself across the great room.

Another time, I returned from work to enter the master bath and "something" had removed about five brushes and combs and lined them up in a perfect line across the vanity.

Another time I was in the kitchen doing dishes, wiping the counter, etc. I turned my back on the sink and turned back to find the sponge and its metal holder sitting smack in the middle of the aluminum sink. If it had fallen, it wouldn't have been so perfect, and would have made the metal on metal clang. There have been lots of other items mysteriously moved here.

There have been footsteps across the dining room, boldly too. Since about our sixth month here, knocks on the wall and doors opening by themselves. My bedroom door slammed one night when we were trying to fall asleep. And twice, I've heard a man's voice, very near, go "Pssst!" Lots of times I've asked my hubby, "What did you say?" when I heard a man's voice, and he swears he's said nothing.

Also, we have a china cabinet that won't stay closed. It's opened right in front of us. Right now, I have it pinned closed with twist ties. It has a history. My grandmother had rental units and one group of renters my mom would only describe to me as "some strange cult" left a bunch of furniture in the rental. The cabinet was one of the pieces. I've heard a lot of raps on the wall directly opposite the wall it sits on.

Sorry so long. This is sort of a condensed version, though.

Mine Road

Date received: October 1997

This story did not actually take place in a coal mine, but it is related to the industry.

22 Mine Road. A legend is told about the road that your car will be pushed up it if you stop. This is bull, but that is just one of the urban legends that has risen up around the true story of the mine road. The story is as follows. This is how the legend was told to me by my grandfather.

22 Mine Road is located between Williamson, West Virginia and Logan, West Virginia. During the twenties, coal was mined by hand. Coal miners would drill holes in mine walls and fill them with dynamite, then they would scoop the rubble into carts.

One day, John (made up, of course) was late for his shift, so he kissed his wife and ran out the door. Looking at the kitchen table, his wife Mary noticed that he had left his lunch sitting there. She took it upon herself to take it to John.

Mary wrapped herself in her best coat and left the house, determined to catch John before he went underground. She walked for some time, unable to find him. By now, she was at the base of 22 Mine Road.

Knowing that John had already started work, Mary stalked up the hill, hoping to find someone who would give her dear husband his lunch. She never made it.

A rumbling shook the mountain path. Mary knew that this was a dynamite blast and was not worried. She was familiar with them. Ahead of her, she saw a cloud of dust. Again, she was not worried.

Seconds later, two mules with fully loaded carts came hurtling down the mountain. Mary was in their path and could not get out of the way.

Later, as John and the other workers came out of the mine in search of the mules that had been spooked by the blast, they found Mary's coat torn and bloody in the middle of the road. They did not find Mary.

This ends the history of 22 Mine Road. Following is the story as it was told to me this morning by my grandfather. I cannot verify the story, but I don't think Grampa would make it up.

My grandfather used to drive a coal truck for a living. He had no place to park it at home, so he would leave it locked up on 22 Mine Road and drive his pickup home.

One night, he did this. He was cruising down the road when his pickup died. He was near the base of 22 Mine Road, so he decided to go back and take his chances with parking the coal truck. One problem, he had no flashlight.

He started up the road and noted a glow against the trees in the middle distance. It was green and it was moving towards him. Grampa thought it was a car, so he didn't think twice about walking towards it. Soon, he found out how wrong he was.

The light, Grampa found, was coming from a sphere that floated a few feet of the ground. Not being afraid of much, and curious of what this was, Grampa took a step towards it. The sphere moved back. Grampa stepped forward again. Again, the light moved backwards.

Grampa ran towards the sphere and still it kept the distance between them. The light was bright enough to light the path. This continued for some time, until Grampa found himself looking at his coal truck. The light faded and Grampa never had an experience like this again.

Was this the ghost of "Mary," leading my Grandfather to safety? Or was it a guardian spirit or angel? He does not know. (Actually, he doesn't care, if he can't touch it, he doesn't believe it.)

Hope you liked it. I'm currently looking for somebody who can tell me more about Mary. Her ghost is supposed to wander the road, I think. If I find a story about her, I'll post it too if anyone is interested.

Church Ghost

Date posted: November 1997

I'm reposting this story for all of you who have been following the current stories of the church I used to belong to, which includes the haunted YMCA which was an annexed building to this church. This church is still considered to be haunted by those who work there. Here is a story I originally posted months ago.

When I was in my teens and very active in my church, I was in charge of decorating the church basement for a Halloween party we were having that night. Yes, that was back in the days when everyone didn't feel the need to be so P.C. and the church didn't have any problem with a Halloween party. I was given the key to the church since no one was going to be there to let us in that day. My friend and I let ourselves in and very carefully locked the door behind us.

We proceeded to the basement to put up the decorations. All was very quiet and we had no music playing. Suddenly, we realized that we could hear footsteps overhead. The footsteps went round and round the sanctuary that was directly overhead. We crept to the phone, which, thank God, was very nearby, and called the police for help. We did not go upstairs or try to confront whoever or whatever it was because, quite frankly, we were terrified.

Very quickly, a nice police officer arrived and as we let him in, he could tell by our faces that we were very upset. He did a most thorough search of the church, starting on the second floor and working his way down to the sub-basement. He even opened the back doors of the church and flagged down some passing garbage men to ask if they had seen anyone lurking about. They hadn't.

He assured us all was well and we went back down to the basement so he could take our names and some info for the report he would later write up.

Unexpectedly, as we quietly sat there talking, the footsteps started up again, directly over our heads. I know my eyes were as big as saucers as they met the policeman's equally big eyes. My friend's teeth literally began to chatter she was so afraid. There was a moment of stunned silence and he said, very calmly, "I don't know about you, but I'm getting out of here."

And we were out of there before you could blink. I even left my coat behind to be picked up later. I like to think now, from the safety of many years later, that we looked like a Marx Brothers moment, all of us trying to get out the door at the same time. I often wonder what he wrote on his report.

Years later, my father, who was a Scout Master at that church and held his meetings in the sub-basement, told me it was not unusual to hear unexplained noises there. He too had heard the footsteps.

We know for a fact that one man did die in the sanctuary. In fact, he died in my father's arms. An older gent, he had a heart attack just upon arriving for church and as he fell, my father caught him. The man was not a member of our church and no one had ever seen him before. But we can no longer remember if his death came before or after we heard the footsteps.

This church had an "annex" which seemed equally haunted but was, somehow, more sinister—no one would ever go in there alone. The footsteps in the church scared us only because we knew they did not belong there, but they didn't really cause the feeling of fear that was often felt in the "annex" part of the church. The annex was an old YMCA and I'm sure it had many, many stories of its own to tell. Strangely enough, the only "ghost" that I actually saw there was female. I'd sure love to know the story behind that restless spirit.

Cookie Ghost

Date received: January 1998

Hi, all. I posted this story about two years ago to A.F.G.S., and I cannot find my original post. Still, I'll write as much as I remember because I found it rather humorous.

A group of my friends and I got together one night for a story-telling session. Any kind of story was permitted, but since one guy, Josh, freaked everyone out with his encounter with a guardian spirit in a state park, we all decided to make a ghosty kind of night. All of the stories got sort of scary, so one of my friends, a perpetual optimist, thought she'd lighten the mood. Here is, more or less, what Kitty told.

Kitty had a friend who lived in a large, plantation-style Southern house. There was a cottage down the hill from the house that her parents used to rent out. Anyway, they first rented it to a family of a husband, wife, and small girl.

At this point, the view shifts to the wife of the new inhabitants. She and her husband and daughter used to leave on the weekends to go into town to do shopping and other errands. After they had lived in the cottage for a few weeks, they came home one Sunday and discovered that there were fresh-baked cookies in the oven. The wife thought, "Am I going crazy? Nobody got any ingredients out to make cookies. Did they?" So she asked her husband and the family up the hill, who both replied in the negative.

This kept occurring, and they had to assume that it was a ghost or some sort of spirit, since they could never find anyone in the act of playing a joke on them. No other manifestations were made apparent, but they could count on fresh cookies whenever they went out for an afternoon. After a while, they decided to move because they were afraid of other manifestations occurring which would have the potential to scare their daughter. So they moved away, and two gentlemen rented the cottage.

At this point, we return the camera to focus on the parents of Kitty's friend, who had not told the gentlemen that there was a ghost in the cottage. They noticed that these men stayed on for about a year, and so they wondered if the ghost was showing itself. One day the mother who lived in the "big house" went down to ask how things were. When nothing was forthcoming, she asked, "You haven't, um, had any unusual experiences happen in the past year, have you?"

One of the men just looked at her and said, "Oh, you mean the ghost? Oh, we love him. He makes cookies for us at least once a week."

Happy haunting!

Convenience Store Ghost

Date posted: May 1995

Hiya, it's been a while since I posted but here's a true ghostly tale from the convenience store-checkered streets of Tucson, AZ, The Circle K Phantom, as told to me by Gwen.

My friend Gwen used to do the clerk thing at various convenience stores in town to get herself through college. This time period of jumping around from 7-Eleven to Quick Mart to Circle Ks lasted roughly from 1990 to 1992. Gwen's first gig was at a little Circle K in a somewhat quiet neighborhood on the south side of town. Her shift lasted from 10:00 PM to 6:00 AM. Yup, you guessed it—the graveyard shift.

At first things were somewhat busy. A road construction crew was building an off ramp to one of the main freeways in town at night and so Gwen experienced brisk business from the husky and burly folk. The work was done about a month later and business during that time reduced significantly.

In order to pass the time, Gwen brought in a small clock radio to listen to late night talk shows. Occasionally during mopping detail, Gwen would tune the radio to top 40 radio. She noticed over time that the radio's volume would go down slowly until it was inaudible. Gwen would then simply walk over to the radio and turn it up again. Again, over a period of about an hour, the volume would go down.

As the days went by, Gwen began to notice that the radio would completely shut off when she tuned to the Top 40 station, despite the fact that the radio was brand new. She took it back home, where it operated perfectly. So then she took in a boom box and the very same phenomena occurred. However, Gwen would hear signals and "noise" coming from the stereo even though it was shut off and sometimes even when it was unplugged. She eventually took the stereo home, where it worked fine. Spooked but far from calling in parapsychologists, Gwen decided not to listen to top 40 or any radio at all and the occurrences stopped.

A few months into her employment at Circle K, Gwen began to get the feeling that she was being watched. She had just stopped dating a very possessive man at the time and she confided in me that she felt that he might be stalking her. There were times she felt that she was being watched from across the street. One night, she looked out the window and saw a small man who appeared to be hunched over sitting at a bus stop bench across the street. The man appeared to be looking into right into her direction. Later, she figured that the man had been sitting there for about three hours.

A few hours before dawn, a police officer came in for his nightly dose of coffee and snacks. Gwen asked him if he could go speak to the man who was sitting across the street because she felt uncomfortable with his peculiar behavior. The cop looked at her oddly and asked, "What man?" Gwen, the image of the man staring her right in the face, pointed and said "That man." The cop insisted that he could not see anyone although it was plain as day for Gwen. The cop promised he'd be on the lookout for anyone suspicious and left. Gwen swears that the man disappeared moments after the cop left.

The man would reappear from time to time and Gwen would attempt to take a picture of him or go outside to try to confront him. By this time, she was convinced that something ghostly was going on. After a time, the man wasn't seen by Gwen ever again. Yet strange occurrences still went on. At first it was a few strange noises—some bumps and clicks—then it was things falling off shelves and the video game getting unplugged. Pretty soon Gwen felt like a babysitter for a bored ghost. She eventually got used to it and called the ghost "George," her dead brother whom she believed the ghost was.

One night, the milk guy came in with a shipment. Gwen went back to the rear of the store to open up the refrigeration storage area. Gwen was bored so she decided to chat with the guy and help him unload. Expecting him to come through the rear, she was startled when he came through the front. He looked at her a little curiously and asked her, "What's the deal with your boss?" Not having the foggiest idea what he was talking about, Gwen responded "What boss?" The milk guy explained that there was a strange looking man in a Circle K shirt with a sour look on his face. The guy then went on to describe the man as having a hunchback and glasses, the same as the man across the street. Gwen just about peed in her pants upon hearing this and went out to look at the counter only to find no one there.

After that night, Gwen decided that her days were numbered at the Circle K and she gave her two weeks' notice, partly because of the ghostly stuff but mostly because she got a job at a 7-Eleven during regular day hours. The day before she left, she found herself very tuckered out and tired around 4:00 AM. She did not look forward to the fact that she would start her new job that very day at 8:00.

Around 4:30 AM, a group of young ruffians came into the store and bought a variety of cokes, candies, and nachos. They stood around the magazine section and chomped away at their goodies. Gwen watched them carefully but soon found herself falling asleep. A few moments passed and she fell asleep. Maybe five minutes passed and she was awakened by the noise of a paper boat of nachos hitting the floor. The boys were nowhere in sight and there was a big cheesy mess on the floor. Gwen looked up at one of those circular mirrors to see if the boys were up to some kind of scheme and she noticed a dark figure for an instant. Gwen went out to the aisles to investigate but found no one and nothing.

About a year after her stint with Circle K, Gwen ran into her old boss at a bus stop. They chatted for a bit and the boss mentioned that the store was shut down about three months after a big AM-PM opened up and pushed it out of business. He also mentioned that they could never keep anyone to do the graveyard shift and that he thought Gwen worked it the longest—four months. He also mentioned that she broke the record set by the guy who worked it before her, a small, nearsighted, hunchbacked man named Jerry who had been shot and killed in an attempted robbery a month before Gwen started work there.

Coon Hunt

Date received: April 2002

I have written a story in this site once before, and was dismayed at the way it turned out. The story was Apache Hill. Even though the writing was horrendous, it was still definitely true, 100% so.

The story I am going to relate happened to my father, a man whom I have nothing but the utmost respect for, who taught me to never lie. This was a pet peeve of his. He hated liars, so when he related this story to me I knew I had heard the truth and a very strange tale.

When I was about fifteen years of age, Dad used to coon hunt all the time, not just for sport but for fur money as well. There would have many sad Christmases if it hadn't been for Dad's coon hunting and trapping on the side. Anyway, this one particular night he was out hunting across the highway from a ranch called Granite Hills in or very near Llano, Texas. He had been out for about an hour or so, and he could hear his hounds trailing on a coon, and from the sound of them it was a hot trail too.

He started heading their direction when all of a sudden they hushed up altogether. Now, that is not unusual in itself, since hounds will do that occasionally for a minute or two, but this lasted longer than that. He soon heard their feet hitting the ground as they came running full blast back to him. Over the hill they came, and they never slowed down a whit but continued right on past Dad with their tails between their legs, running as fast as they could right back to the truck dad had parked down the road.

Dad stood there for a minute wondering what the hell that was all about. They had never done that before. Dad being Dad decided to investigate, so he walked over the hill, and there before him was a large patch of ground torn all to pieces and with what looked like a large pig torso in the middle of it. He would have looked further, but right at that moment it got cold and a voice as if someone were right there beside him said, "Leave now!" He turned around right then and went back to the truck.

When he got back to the truck, he was surprised to find his hounds already in there cage waiting for him and shaking in their skins. Well, he had caught a coon earlier that night and so decided to go ahead and skin it before he left. He was halfway through skinning it when a freezing wind blew across the back of his neck and a voice like someone standing right behind him said, "Get out!"

He spun around with his knife in his hand, and if anyone had been there, their insides would have been their outsides. There was no one there but Dad definitely did not feel alone. He left the coon hanging where it was, jumped in his truck, and barreled out of there. He never went back to the ranch.

I always wondered why he would never hunt there, whereas before this when I was younger we hunted there all the time and have pulled some big coons out of there. Mom did say that she remembers this because that was the night he came home from hunting as white as a sheet, and would not talk about it for the longest time.

Copy Cat

Date posted: March 1999

The things that I want to tell you about are more like short stories really, because they never lasted very long. Since I was very small, strange things have happened at my Mom's and Dad's house. I've never actually seen a ghost there, but, well, you decide.

One night around 2:00 AM I was in bed and I saw the hall light go on and knew my mom was up, so I got up and we were talking. Now, from the hallway I could see the kitchen. The light was off in there but you could still see into it, and I saw my Dad in his work uniform with his back to me drinking a cup of something. Well, my dad doesn't go to work until about 5:00 AM. I asked my mom, "Why is Daddy up so early?" She looked and said, "I don't know," so we went in, turned on the light, and he was gone. We went in their bedroom and my dad was sound asleep.

One night my sister had a boyfriend over. It was very late and my parents are very strict, so when she saw my dad get out of bed and go into the kitchen, she and her boyfriend hid and waited for him to go back to bed. Well, he never came back out, so my sister went to look in the kitchen and he wasn't there.

I was dating a real jerk at one time and my folks were on vacation. We stayed at their house and slept in the front room on the floor. We both folded our clothes neatly and went to sleep, but when we woke up his clothes were thrown all over the house and mine were still neat. He said he would never sleep there again. Guess the ghost didn't like him too much.

When I was a teenager, my friend Danielle was living with us at one point and we shared my room. Our friend Theresa stayed over one night and she and I slept in the front room while Danielle took the bedroom. I'm a very light sleeper and I remember a light waking me up. I sat up to see what it was... it was Danielle in the refrigerator. All I could see was this blonde ponytail bopping up and down like she was searching for something. I looked at the clock it was 3:00 AM. I thought, "Geez, what an oinker," and went back to sleep. The next day I asked her about it but she said she never got up at all. Then I thought about it. If she was in the fridge, I would have seen her whole body, not just her hair, because of the way the fridge opens. It was opened from the opposite side.

Before I got married and moved out I used to come home and walk to my parents' bedroom if my mom wasn't in the front room. If my mom was napping I would just walk in. My mom always knew it was me because footsteps echoed in that house, and she would wake up before I got to the room. Now I'm not there anymore, but during the day when she's alone she still hears the footsteps. It sounds like someone's walking quickly to her room and she lies there waiting for me to burst in, but the footsteps stop right outside the door. When she gets up to see if it's me, nobody's there.

So what do you think? Spooky, eh? If they do have a ghost it doesn't bother anyone; it just takes on the image of the people in my family. My parents did find out later that an elderly woman died in our house in 1970.

Cult House

Date received: March 1997

The area where I grew up in Northern Delaware had the same sort of urban legends, rumors, and general teenage superstition that I think every community does. When I was in high school, there was one particularly prevalent story about a mansion located in the woods of the Brandywine Valley. This house was actually just north of the Pennsylvania border. Everyone called it Cult House.

Now, I'm not sure how this rumor started. I do know that some of my friends' fathers could remember the same story involving the same location being told when they were in high school.

According to local legend, this mansion is supposedly owned and operated by a "Satanic Cult." In some versions, the "Cult" is associated with a prominent Delaware family involved in the chemical industry. The window panes are in the shape of inverted crosses. The trees that line the road running along the side of the house grow at a very distinct angle away from the house, in some areas away from their main light source. Most interestingly, there is a "guard house" on the grounds that houses a fleet of red pickup trucks. If you drive past the house too often, one or several of the trucks will come out of the house and chase you away. No matter how close it gets, you will never be able to catch a glimpse of the driver's face.

There is one particular tree along the road that runs past the house that has exposed roots. The roots form the perfect shape of a human skull. It is said that years ago, police found the remains of a sacrificial victim nestled inside the tree. Reports conflict on whether the victim was human or animal. According to the legend, a human sacrifice is performed on the grounds every Halloween.

Well, that's the rumor. Here is my personal experience with "Cult House." I have been occasionally driving by the place with friends and researching its history for about seven years now. The window panes actually are in the shape of inverted crosses. This seems to be not necessarily intentional—it may just be how those particular panes are shaped. The trees do grow at an extreme angle away from the house and in some places they do seem to grow away from the main light source. This phenomenon stops once you get about one-quarter mile past the house.

There is a guard house and there are red trucks. They have actually followed me before on two occasions. The first was at night, and the truck's lights were off. Amazing, because there are no streetlights, and the trees allow in no moonlight. I couldn't understand how the driver was able to even stay on the road. I was behind it at first. The truck pulled over and waited for me to pass. It then pulled out and followed me until I was several miles from the house. I had one passenger in the car, and you can imagine the state we were in. We were scared to death, but really excited!

The next time was also at night, but with a different friend. After we had driven past the guard house several times, we noticed that we were being followed by a red truck. We hadn't seen it even come onto the road. We never saw the driver's face. Again, we were followed until we were several miles from the house, then the truck just pulled over to the side of the road. Again, the headlights were off. I have never seen anyone entering or exiting the main house or the guard house. I know the trucks are housed at the guard house, because at least five are usually visible in the driveway.

The "skull tree" does look frighteningly like a human skull. I have never found any newspaper accounts confirming that remains of any kind were found in the tree. I have been able to find absolutely no evidence of sacrificial rites being performed during Halloween or at other times, according to local records.

There are a few other unexplained things about the house. First of all, the road that runs past the house is not on any map that I've ever seen, and believe me, I've looked. The two roads that "Cult House Road" connects are on the map, but the road itself is missing. It has no visible street sign indicating its name. I believe that it is a public road because it has road signs and is not actually on the property of the house, which sits about one-quarter of a mile back from the road. The county records office can produce no title for a house in that area matching the description.

The local paper wanted to run a Halloween feature on the legend, hopefully bringing out the facts and cutting down on some of the traffic on the small rural road. The city desk editor of the paper, a friend of mine, said that the paper had obtained a phone number for the house somehow and called to schedule an interview. They explained that they wanted to "debunk" the legend once and for all. She said they were rudely refused by a person who would not even give his name. The paper staff was surprised because they had assumed that the owners would want to stop the rumors.

Lastly, I'd like to give a few of my own impressions of the place. I'm not prepared to say that everything said about the house is true. I can only rely on my own observations. The place definitely has an oppressive air about it. Several of my friends have been near panic at just being in its vicinity. I know one girl who believed she was in danger of becoming possessed after being near the house. She said the spirit she felt was a female victim of some sort of ritual that had been performed on those grounds. She claimed no previous knowledge of the legends surrounding the house.

Often, I've thought I've seen people moving through the trees near the house. When I look again, they're always gone. I have been chased on a public road by their guards. My friends and I have all seen animals in the woods and on the road that we cannot identify. That may have nothing to do with the house, but it sure contributes to the "weirdness" of the environment. I don't know how to properly explain it, but once you've turned onto Cult House road, you feel as if you've entered another dimension. Nothing feels normal. Again, this could all be due to the power of suggestion. Personally, I think there is something going on in the house… I'm just not sure what it is.

Old Witch Blaney

Date posted: October 1997

As a young boy of eleven I ventured with some friends to visit a cemetery. We felt very daring as the cemetery was a mile outside of town and very isolated. This was not some midnight excursion; it was just after midday on an extremely hot August day. In fact, the weather had broken all kind of local records due to the temperature and lack of rain.

I remember clearly that I was with three girls of approximately my age. I was a near-stranger in the town, just there for the holiday with my parents and brothers. I had made new friends of these girls, who seemed to delight in teasing us "foreigners" and playing kiss, chase, and dare type of games.

We wandered around in the cemetery reading out the names and playing hide and seek or chase, then played a few dares. The girls got away with giggly peeks of their underwear, or swearing, or hanging from trees. Then I was dared to stand on a concrete slab-covered, slightly raised tomb and chant three times "Old Witch Blaney I'm not scared of you."

Fine, I thought, no problem. I promptly stood as required and made the chant. I remember the gravestones and the concrete slab were devilishly hot from the sun. The girls went silent and were totally in awe of the brave deed I had performed. I recall that one of the girls then asked wasn't I frightened to say such a thing. I of course replied no and that I had never heard of Old Witch Blaney. Thus the girls with hushed voices told me the tale. It was not a particularly frightening tale, not now that is, but at the time in a cemetery being told by three locals who obviously believed the story, it had me worried to say the least.

Mrs. Blaney was an old woman who had outlived her husband and only son, both of whom had died within a year or so of each other, although none present could recall from what they had died. Mrs. Blaney then suffered from the loneliness and poverty of living alone as a widow in rural Ireland in the sixties. She would often be seen gathering wood in the lanes and woods of the area to use as firewood, the only fuel she used.

She rented a tiny plot of land of approximately half an acre in which she grew her potatoes and some vegetables that were her main sustenance. Her income was a tiny state pension that paid the rent on her cottage and land and little else.

She earned some cash from midwifery, laying out the dead for her neighbours, and some healing. Doctors were still far too expensive for the common people. Years later, I heard that probably a large portion of her money came from illegal abortion, but that was probably rumor.

With working outdoors her skin became tough and wrinkled, she was terribly poor so her clothes were quite tattered, and due to her healing concoctions and midwifery, etc. she was whispered to be a witch. Out of her earshot she was referred to as Old Witch Blaney.

Mrs. Blaney had one major fault—she regularly get extremely drunk, at good old Irish wakes to which she was invited after laying out the dead. She spent a good portion of the income from her healing and midwifery on alcohol.

Now, in rural Ireland it was not becoming for a woman to be seen roaring drunk in the streets, and so the local Gardie (police) had the chore of picking her up and putting her into one of the two tiny cells in the police station that doubled as the police sergeant's home.

This is where the story turns strange. It is alleged that although Mrs. Blaney was regularly picked up and placed in the cell in the evening, she was never there in the morning. The police sergeant was forever trying to puzzle how she was always found at home in her own bed in the morning, with the police cell still locked and empty.

It is to be noted that Mrs. Blaney and the police sergeant were not the best of friends, as he would suffer terrible abuse from her whenever she laid eyes on him.

One night Mrs. Blaney was again drunk and was particularly foul mouthed regarding the sergeant, and apparently his inability to father children, when she was arrested and brought to the cells. In the morning, the sergeant went to look in the cell and sure enough she was gone. He and another officer went to her home to officially release her and do the paperwork. However, when they got to her home they found her dead in bed. There was an investigation and, I presume, a post mortem, etc., the cause of death being natural causes. The policeman was interrogated regarding how she got home, but no answer was ever found. Knowing the local finance, or lack thereof, it is very likely she just picked the lock and went home. Why she would wait and relock it was another mystery, unless she knew it caused the sergeant some concern.

When Mrs. Blaney was buried, many of the locals attended as she had no family, and they set about making her tiny grave as attractive as possible with a small wooden cross and plants and flowers.

However, Mrs. Blaney was spotted several times with a bundle of firewood on her back in the small lanes around the area. Allegedly she was also heard once or twice bad mouthing the Sergeant, as was her way.

Somehow, the police sergeant was able to use some funds and organized that she had a small raised tomb erected over her grave, into which was placed the heavy concrete lid, perhaps to stop her escaping. Mrs. Blaney was never seen again, but several incidents of mischief were pinned on her name and a legend formed that she was trying to escape from her tomb.

After I had been told this mildly scary story, we went back to the grave and I was again dared to stand on the concrete and recite "Old Witch Blaney I'm not scared of you" three times. This time I declined, just in case. However, the girls began to insist, calling me coward, etc. At that moment it started to rain. Great big blobs of rain began to slowly fall, then more and more. Suddenly we heard a tremendous CRACK and a puff of cement dust rose up from a huge crack that had appeared in the concrete slab.

Now, I do not know the world record for the one mile sprint but I bet I had it well beaten that day.

Years after, when I was an adult, I returned and went to look at the grave. There was still the huge crack with an opening large enough to put your hand inside. Strangely, I never did put my hand in.

Of course I can hear you all say that it was just the cold water on the extremely hot concrete, and well, it could have been. But even now as an adult I cannot bring myself to stand on a grave.

Don't know what you think about this daft tale, which happens to be absolutely true, but I have further tales that I can relate with more supernatural twists, also very true. If I get a few replies I will upload them.

Ghost Lights

Date received: May 1998

My father had always told me about these "lights" that dance whenever someone dies. They start in the family graveyard, go up in the field, and then back to the graveyard. Until this past March, only a few people had seen this.

On March 23, 1998 my father died. My sister flew into Virginia to make the drive with me to West Virginia. We were of course going to the homestead, which has been in the family for over 200 years and where my dad was living. We started up the mountain around midnight and lo and behold, as soon as we arrived at the top there were the lights.

There is nothing around so no way were they from any kind of interference or light pollution. In the center were a red light and a green light, and on each side of them were two white lights. They were dancing all around the field and were starting to go to the graveyard. We stayed up until around 2:00 AM and watched until the last one started going down.

The next night my other two sisters arrived from New Mexico and again the lights were dancing. My other sister and I had been watching them since the sun went down. We were all crying because it was as if they were "welcoming" Dad.

Thursday night was the night for the wake. We buried Dad in the old graveyard. We had told everyone in the family that the lights were dancing, and after the wake the whole family went back to the farm to watch. This time there were two red lights in the center and three white lights on each side.

My uncle, Dad's brother, kept asking if one of the lights had left for the other field. Well, they hadn't, until that night. All of a sudden one of the red lights took off and shot across the sky and disappeared behind the next hill. We felt the second red light was Dad because he had red hair. I know it might sound silly but instead of being scared of these lights it was comforting to think that it was Dad and he was being welcomed by our ancestors.

Bathroom Arm

Date posted: September 1994

I have been reading ghost stories for a while now, and see that my little experience is nothing compared to some of those by others in the group. But I must say, this happening is one of the scariest I have ever had.

First, I have to say I have always been interested in the paranormal and unexplainable, but have always been skeptical. I have never had any strange experiences like this anyplace else. I have been up during late hours before and have spent a lot of time alone in other places and late nights at friend's homes. I have never seen or imagined seeing things in other places and I have never been scared or even been thinking of seeing ghosts. Nothing strange has ever happened until I moved into this house. But even to this day, I still wonder about what I have experienced and if there is a "real" explanation for the things I have seen.

This is a bit long, but please bear with me. I want to give you some background and go into some details. These are experiences I have truly had and relate them as I remember them.

Since I have moved into this house, about eight years ago now, there have always been little things that I have wondered about. Frequently, while sitting in my basement and watching television, I would see things out of the corner of my eye. I used to have this ball light at the bottom of the stairway to my basement. Twice, I saw what looked like some kind of cloud, about the height of a figure, but wider, move from just under the light up the stairs. After I changed the light fixture, this never happened again.

Then, while sitting in the same place, I occasionally saw something move across the carpet in the room on my left. This happened on several occasions. I tried to explain it as light from a car or a reflection off my glasses, but there are no places for light to get into the basement on that side and since this only happened occasionally, it just wouldn't be practical for it to be a reflection off my glasses. I have been through three different televisions, so it could not be a reflection from that. Later, while sitting in another part of the room, with a house full of people, I saw this moving across the carpet again. This both interested me and spooked me at the same time, knowing I saw this from somewhere else this time. The movement has always been from the front of the house to the back, never the other way.

In my bedroom on the first floor, after I put in an overhead fan, at times I thought I could hear low voices, as if in a large room behind a closed door.

Well, I always put these things aside in my mind thinking I was just imagining them. My biggest scare came when a friend of mine was over late one night. We were into a long computer session, as I have frequently done with friends on the weekends. We had been talking about some weird things like backwards masking on records and the Beatles mystery in the songs. I'm sure that didn't help matters.

Anyway, a little after 4:00 AM, I went upstairs to the bathroom leaving my friend downstairs to play with the computer. I was thinking in my mind that when I went back down there, I'd ask him if he had any ghost experiences. Anyway, while I was washing my hands, I saw this arm beside me. I remember thinking my buddy was trying to scare me. I quickly turned around to startle him, but all I saw then was an empty bathroom with the door closed behind me.

I jerked my head back around, looking in the mirror over the sink. Looking in the mirror, I glanced over my right shoulder: nothing. I then looked at my own face, with my hair now in front of my eyes from the startled jerk of my head when I turned. There was nothing.

I quickly dried my hands, opened the door, and quickly headed downstairs. My friend could tell something was really wrong. I told him I saw something in the bathroom. I told him I saw an arm, a forearm. I remember it was beautifully colored, like the vivid color of an old Technicolor movie and the skin was smooth, like that of a beautiful young woman. I don't remember a head or a body, just seeing the forearm.

My friend and I talked for about fifteen minutes, and then he was leaving. I was still shaken, and it took all the courage in me to move through my kitchen toward the sink to open my garage door. It was getting too close to the bathroom down the hall for my comfort. We talked outside for about another twenty minutes. I did not want to go back into the house. When he left, I left too, driving around for about two hours until it was daylight. I then went home and went to sleep.

After this incident, I thought about these other things that I just considered imagination. I couldn't sleep with my bedroom door open after that—as if closing the door would really protect me from a spirit. I guess I just didn't want to accidentally see anything. And even though I had to be at work by 6:00 AM, I wouldn't get up until at least 5:00 AM. I felt safe during the day, and was persistent on having lights on in the house.

I told a number of friends about this. Two of them said they both felt an unusual feeling in one particular room. Another friend said he also felt strange in that same room. A couple of girlfriends of his were over one time, and one of them related to him that she felt uncomfortable in my house. She knew nothing of what had happened. As an experiment, another of my buddy's friends, who knew nothing of any of this, was asked to walk through every room in my house. Afterwards, I asked him if he felt uncomfortable or strange in any room. He said not really, except for maybe in this one room—the same room that everyone else felt strange in.

I told a few people of these happenings. Some believed and related their own experiences, while some thought I was just a little goofy. Nothing happened for about six or seven months, and I finally settled down, being able to sleep well at nights and with the bedroom door open. Then one evening, I saw this scurrying across the carpet in the room next to where I was watching television. But this was different than other times; I actually saw somewhat of a pressing down of the carpet and the movement was in the opposite direction this time, from the back of the house to the front.

About a month ago, some friends were over and we were messing around in the computer room. While someone was showing me how to get around on the Internet, I saw this somewhat glistening thing near the upper part of the room near the computer room. It looked like light reflecting off some crumpled aluminum foil. I just took it as seeing things. A couple hours later, one of my friends, the same one who was with me the night of my "sighting," looked in the same direction I saw the reflection, and appeared a bit startled. I asked him what was wrong. At first he said nothing, but then said he saw kind of a shadow up near the ceiling. It was in the same place I saw my glistening object.

Spirit Fingers

Date received: April 1998

Hi! My whole family on both my mother and father's side seem to be magnets for spirits. Every one of my relatives have either seen or felt something that they could not explain. We used to sit around and share our experiences with one another. I have had many different experiences myself.

Anyway, the one that I wish to relate to you is the one that stands out most in my mind, not only because I had very direct contact with the spirit, but because it was the only one that was definitely not benevolent. First a little background of previous experiences from others in my family.

Since before I was born, my grandparents on my father's side lived in this old stone two story house that was haunted. At night heavy footsteps could be heard upstairs walking around. Cold wind would blow upstairs even when no one was there and the rotary phone upstairs would dial all by itself. That used to really freak me out. I hated to be in that house by myself because I always felt a horrible presence.

My mother once saw a large man that looked just like the previous owner staring at her as she walked down the stairs. An old woman who was presumed to be his wife was also seen on several occasions. It was said that she absolutely hated children when she was alive. My cousin when she was about 11 felt an unknown force try to strangle her. She never set foot back into that house.

Now to my own experience. When I was 10 years old, we lived only two houses down, so in the summer I would go swimming a lot in the pool with my other two cousins. Well, we needed towels so I went upstairs to the large wardrobe that was in the hallway. As soon as I opened the door and reached for the towels, a horrible cold feeling came over me, even though it was 90 degrees outside and hot in the house. Then I felt a hand grab my shoulder and squeeze very hard, like it was trying to hurt me. I struggled to get free and when I turned around no one was there.

Needless to say, I ran down the stairs as fast as my feet could carry me. I didn't tell anyone because at this time I didn't know the history of the house or my family. What made me know for sure that it wasn't in my imagination was that I had bruises in the shape of four fingers on my shoulder and it ached for a few days after. Whatever it was had a death grip on me. After that I would never go upstairs again without someone with me, and I never again stayed the night. I was very happy when they moved away from there.

I have had many experiences since then, but this story is long as it is. If anyone would like to share stories, just email me and I'd be happy to! I am a very firm believer and I keep a very open mind about it.

Thanks for letting me share.

Cry Baby Lane

Date posted: March 1999

Back in the late '50s to early '60s there used to be an orphanage run by the Catholic Church in Raleigh. One horrible night a fire broke out in the orphanage, taking several young children to their death. After the fire the Church decided not to rebuild, and after a period of time all remnants of the orphanage were removed. Brush and weeds slowly took over the area.

As the surrounding neighborhood began to develop, so did tales of the fire. They say on quiet summer nights you can hear the whimpering and crying of babies. Years later when I heard the story, a couple of friends tried to get me to go out to where the old orphanage stood on a quiet night. Now, that area is no longer the safest area in Raleigh, and being more afraid of things that lurked in the night than things that go bump in the night, I declined, with the promise that we would go the following afternoon. Neither of us had been there before, so the next day we were off on our little adventure.

We arrived at the site, and followed a well-beaten path to where the old building once stood. Like I had mentioned earlier, the property had been over taken with weeds and brush. But where the orphanage once stood was a bare spot about 100 feet across with no grass, weeds, or bushes. On the ground there were a couple of footprints that went a couple of feet into the spot, then doubled back. We also noticed a rabbit run out of the weeds and completely circle around the spot instead of crossing it. We circled the spot a couple of times, none of us too willing to cross it. Soon we all had the feeling that it would be best if we left, so we did.

But a few days later, my curiosity got the better of me and off I went by myself to Cry Baby Lane. I went down the path, determined I was going to walk across the bare spot. I hesitated a bit before stepping onto the barren ground and took a deep breath.

Just a yard or so into it, I was overtaken by absolute silence. I couldn't hear the wind in the trees, traffic from the nearby highway, nothing. I couldn't even hear my own heartbeat. But I was still stubborn enough to try to make it across. Once I reached the center, I stood still and listened. Just faintly I could hear a crackling noise. It grew louder as the acrid sent of smoke hit my nose. I stood there frozen, half in terror and half in amazement. Suddenly there was the shrill wail of an infant and I ran, and no, not the rest of the way across. I doubled back and didn't stop running till I reached my car.

It was a couple of years later when I gathered enough nerve to go back, but it was too late. As I made my way down the path, I saw bulldozers clearing the area for a new road. A road that I will not drive down.

Dog Ghost

Date received: May 1998

When I was eight years old my parents divorced, and shortly after my father remarried a woman from South Carolina. As he had just retired from the Navy and found there were no jobs to be had, they decided to move near her family in South Carolina, thus separating me from my mother and the tiny private school I grew up in and the ocean I had always lived on.

A few months before the move my stepsisters, stepmother, and I bought my dad a dog for Father's Day. She was a six month old Doberman-German Shepherd mix who we suspect had been badly abused, and since she was free and we were poor we took her even though she had a broken leg.

The puppy and I immediately bonded. We had hour-long games of tag on the beach every day, we sang together and shared everything. She became extremely loyal to me.

Anyway, we all made the cross-country move to South Carolina. For two years she was my only friend.

Finally I got the opportunity to visit my mother in California. I stayed a month, but I was plagued by severe nervousness, sleeplessness, a strange rash, and nightmares about my dog. I should have been having a perfect time home with my friends, in my home, away from the hellish place my stepmother's home became.

When I returned, I learned that my stepsisters had been forbidden to talk about my dog. Although I had asked about her and told them about my nightmares, they always lied and said she was fine, when indeed she had been missing much of the time I was gone.

My dad had taken to tying her to a tree on a choke chain to keep her in the fence and safe. The first time I saw her when I returned home she was on the chain, stinking like dog that had been roaming the street for weeks.

The following morning I went down in my backyard and called her. My dad was in the far corner of the yard burning trash and branches on a new spot, different from his usual burning spot. My dog came to me that morning. She was clean and smelled like she normally should. I remember rubbing her and asking if she felt better now that she had had a bath. We nuzzled each other and then I told her I had to go in and finish my chores. I said, "Sit high," and she sat up on her haunches with her paws up, and I got on my knees and put her paws on my shoulders and we hugged as we often did.

After dinner that evening I went to feed her, when my dad stopped me and told me that she wasn't down there. I asked if she ran off again and he told me know that early that morning he went down to bathe her for me and found her dead at the end of her leash at the tree. She had strangled herself trying to pull off the chain. The new spot my dad was burning on was over her grave.

I protested. I knew I had just talked to her that morning. They all said it was just my imagination, but I couldn't explain it. I still can't. Was it really just my imagination? If this was an encounter with the spiritual world, wow what a solid feeling, what a happy feeling.

I'm thankful for having a last moment with her. I wish I had stayed with her longer. She and I were more closely bonded than I have ever been with anyone. This isn't the only experience I have ever had, but the most vivid. For a while after I had a hard time believing that she was really gone, because I had seen her, held her, smelled her, played with her.

If anyone has any thoughts on this experience I would appreciate hearing them.

Daffodil House

Date posted: March 1999

Call me crazy (hey everyone else does, so why not my spooky friends too?!) but as a teen my friends and I loved exploring abandoned properties. There was a house just outside of town about a half mile off the highway that had intrigued me since childhood and I had to go see it. One afternoon two of my friends agreed that it would be a great place to check out, so we loaded up and went.

It was a typical "creepy old farmhouse" type place made of wood that had begun to rot decades ago. It had dirty, mostly broken windows and a rickety porch. It was two stories high plus an attic. Getting in was no problem; the doors were gone so we just walked on in. There was evidence of other people having been there, as the room we concluded to be the living room was full of empty beer cans and potato chip bags.

Uninterested in these findings, we made our way into the kitchen. It was broad daylight outside but this house was pretty dark inside, adding to the intrigue and creepiness. The kitchen was a wreck and it seemed as though the mice had taken full advantage of whatever had been left there, so we continued on to the dining room.

Finally we saw a set of stairs, the first ones we had seen so far, and up we went. On the third step from the top, I sat my soda can down so we'd be able to remember that's where we came up… I'm glad I had the foresight to do that. We meandered around the top floor and found that it was much brighter and warmer up there, probably because it wasn't under the cover of the low tree branches as the downstairs had been.

We weren't feeling too afraid, just a little uneasy, as we walked around until we got to a large room on the east side. I can't really explain what I felt—mostly I felt as though I wanted to cry. Someone was very sad, that much I could feel. Whoever it was hadn't been ready to die when they did and weren't able to say goodbye and let go.

My friend Matt left the room, stating that he was finding it difficult to breathe, blaming the dust. My friend Maddie was very pale and shaking so we decided it was time to go. We walked around the top floor looking for stairs to the attic, but couldn't find them. We did find a set going down, which we had missed on the first few go-rounds, so down we went... they led to the living room! How was that possible?

We walked around the downstairs peeking in all the little doors for stairs only to find closets. There wasn't a door to get out of the living room, so we went back upstairs and walked around some more. Finally, Maddie spotted the stairs where my soda can was and we happily bounded down them and back into the dining room.

We made our way around the downstairs again just to be sure. The dining room led to the back porch and the kitchen and had stairs to go up, the kitchen only led to the dining room and the living room, the living room only led to the kitchen and the porches. Okay, so where were the stairs we walked down? This was the same room because the mess on the floor was the same and the mantle above the fireplace was the same, so what was the deal here?

We went back upstairs. Maddie stayed at the top of the stairs while Matt and I walked around again in search of the mystery steps we had gone down. We never found them. As Matt and I were walking back toward Maddie, I heard someone in the large bedroom that had made me feel so sad. It sounded like a soft crying and I felt very bad; I felt that we had intruded into this person's life and it was time we left.

Most places we visited, we went back for a second and sometimes third look; however, this place, we didn't. We all felt after we left that maybe whoever was there really just wanted to be left alone and we never went back together.

The very oddest thing is that on Easter Day of the following year, I had this unstoppable urge to go to the house and leave flowers on the porch. I got some daffodils and headed out there only to find my friends Matt and Maddie also had come to bring flowers. We had all had that urge and we all headed out there without the others knowing with a big bouquet of fresh daffodils. Something there had touched each of us, and I will forever feel a connection to that house in the woods and whomever it is who lives in the large room on the east side of the upper floor who seems to like daffodils.

Donner Site

Date received: September 1998

Hi, Obiwan! Congratulations on your new baby! I hope you're having fun.

I was so glad to chance by ghosts.org today and find new stories posted that I thought I'd pester you with this experience I had in the spring. Dealing with some strong impressions I had while visiting an historic place, this could either be viewed as a ghost story, a psychological study, or a report on the effects on the brain of altitude change. I titled it "The Donner Campsite." I can't say for certain what happened while I was there, but I will never forget the feelings I had that day. If you post it, I would welcome the comments of anyone who reads it. Thanks!

P.S.—I have another story posted on your site called "Gentle Ghost."

Anybody familiar with the history of the American West, or who has seen the movie "The Shining," has heard at least vaguely of the Donner Party. This was a group of some ninety pioneers who, in the late fall of 1846, while attempting to emigrate into California, were trapped in the Sierra Nevada Mountains by an early snowfall. They had no choice but to camp high in the mountains and wait out the incredibly vicious winter. Their agony lasted almost six months, nearly half of their number dying of exposure or starvation during that time. As the food supply diminished, some of the living turned to cannibalizing the remains of the dead in order that they might survive. In short, they experienced hardships like few have known, and led a miserable existence huddled in their makeshift cabins and tents which were near what is now called Donner Lake and the city of Truckee, California.

Being a history buff, I focused my interest on the Donners' story for a couple months back in 1992, and read every written account I could find on the subject until I felt as though I knew these long-dead people. Usually I could discuss my extracurricular scholarly pursuits with my egghead, Ph.D. of a boyfriend, but he would have none of this cannibalistic pioneer stuff. I begged him to visit their mountain campsites with me (he was the one with the car), but he would not set foot in that part of the country unless he was wearing skis. So, while I got to spend winters swooshing down the slopes near Donner Lake, I never had the chance to explore the way I would have liked.

Finally last April, while vacationing alone (I had dumped the tweed months before), I decided to spend some time in Reno, Nevada to do a little gambling and soak in some kitsch. The highway from my home in San Francisco to Reno passes by Donner Lake, and although my interest in the topic had waned, I planned to stop and make my first springtime visit. As I wound my way higher into the Sierras, I found myself getting excited, as though I were about to see beloved friends for the first time in years. Self-analysis caused me to suspect altitude sickness, although I had never felt this odd during any of my previous mountain trips.

Half a mile before the lake exit is a scenic overlook with a spectacular view of the beautiful blue water, and of the snow covered peak—Donner Summit—that the emigrants were unable to cross all those years ago. As I stepped out of the car, my first inexplicable thought was, "I can smell them." I snapped a couple pictures, then moved the viewfinder from my eye and just stared at the summit, tears welling up. Then I came out of my daze, chiding myself for being so melodramatic, and drove down to the lake.

The museum associated with the Donner Party and Emigrant Trail should have fascinated me, but my mind was elsewhere as I looked through the personal effects and photographs on display. Even going to two nearby cabin sites didn't stir me much, although I was very aware of the gruesome tales, the death and suffering, associated with each spot. It was a quiet, gorgeous place, if not a little somber, but I did not have a spell like the one I had while staring up at Donner Summit.

Approximately six miles from the lake was a second camp at a creekside where the Donners were believed to have passed that miserable winter. Initially I considered not going out of my way to visit, but deep down felt a draw and turned off of the interstate. Marked simply as a picnic ground, the site is off a two lane highway. It was about 4:30 PM when I pulled in and parked, the sole visitor there. This didn't worry me, as I am used to secluded hikes. I dutifully read the historical markers, and found the beginning of the short and, according to the sign posted, unchallenging trail that circled through the area.

There had been recent visitors on the trail. I noted many varying sizes of sneaker tracks, as well as the imprint of bicycle wheels, in the dirt. At first I walked along with complete confidence. But about a hundred feet in I kept getting the urge to look behind me. It was utterly ridiculous, but I sensed I was not alone. Yet company of the human or other large mammal variety was nowhere to be seen or even heard. My pace quickened. To my right, so small in the distance, was my car, and I yearned for that car. A panic built up within me that I would never leave this place alive. The real life scenario I was in began to take the tone of a waking nightmare, for no apparent reason. Yet I bore ahead.

I reached an old tree with a burnt-out hollow at the base of the trunk that is marked as the site of George and Tamsen Donner's tent (archeological evidence does not support this, however). I took a Polaroid shot of it, but the picture was overexposed, and I was out of film, and, of course, all my film stock was back in the car. As unbelievable as it was to me, if I wanted a picture (and I did), I would have to retrace my steps and possibly endure the terror that was with me the first time around.

After some reflection, I decided that if I did return to the supposed tent site, I would approach via the other half of the trail, which I hadn't yet seen. So I hurried ahead to survey, discovering that the ground there had been saturated by the creek, creating bog-like conditions. Desperate as a stalked animal, I worked my way over some fallen logs, teetering, nearly falling, nearly twisting an ankle, not being my careful old self. For some irrational reason, I wanted off the trail so badly that my usual caution was secondary.

Once on the safety of pavement my mind cleared, and I realized I needed to use the bathroom. Luckily there was one near the car. I went into the women's stall, which thankfully was well kept. While I sat in there, I heard erratic noises in the men's room next door—a scuffling sound, like boots dragging across cement, and then more subtle sounds that reminded me of "tinkering," like someone milling through a toolbox.

There were no trees close to the structure, so I first told myself it was only water pressure in the plumbing. But this was merely a modernized outhouse, lacking even the luxury of a sink. So I rationalized further. It didn't sound like an animal; at any rate, the bathrooms were sealed well enough to prevent such invasion. And there was no reason for a human to be hiding in there. A homicidal maniac would've attacked me by then, a person in trouble would have called for my help. I didn't know what was making those noises, and I wasn't going to find out. I finished up my business with relative composure, considering the directions in which my imagination was headed—had the latrine been built over one of the tent sites? Once back outside, I stopped to listen. The noises were no longer perceptible.

Instead of making the obvious choice of speeding away while I still could, I retrieved a new pack of film from the car and started back to the head of the trail, feeling like I was pressing my luck, yet determined to overcome my nonsensical, raging unease. This time out I began to calm down, though still felt watched. I again found the George Donner Tree, took some pictures, removed a discarded juice bottle from what might have been the hearth, and ran my fingers along the scorch marks that could have been made by a long-dead fire, reflecting on those who had desperately sought warmth decades ago.

Walking back the way I had come, the panic and fear almost vanished. Yet these were only to be replaced by an exceedingly hollow sorrow. "I have never been more alone in my life," I thought to myself. As illogical as it was, I literally felt as though I had no one left in the world. The intense grief that washed over me was, fortunately, my last unsolicited emotion for that day.

I climbed behind the wheel of my car, thankful to be leaving and to have such an efficient means of escape, and proud of myself for not succumbing to whatever was racking my emotions. I sped toward the neon lights of Reno, looking forward to re-entering the land of the living.

I am not sure what caused my feelings to go haywire that afternoon. Maybe all the facts swimming in my head were playing tricks on my subconscious. Perhaps, on this one occasion, despite my love of nature and the trust I have in myself, my solitude had gotten the better of me.

Or maybe other people's strong emotions do imprint themselves on the environment, as some have theorized. If this were the case, the panic I felt over never leaving the camp area alive would have obviously derived from what those people agonized over during the winter of 1846-1847. Furthermore, Tamsen Donner, legendary for her intelligence, resourcefulness, and devotion as a mother and wife, had eventually sent her children to their safety over Donner Summit with a relief party, remaining by her husband's side until his death. After shrouding his body, she was the last person to leave the campsite, walking away alone in hopes of joining her daughters in what is today the state capital of Sacramento. Could I have felt the traces of her probable loneliness and grief floating about amongst the air molecules as I, too, was walking away?

If ghosts do exist, my hope is that those who suffered so much in life are not eternally bound to the place that was their frozen hell on earth. Reflecting on my sojourn at Alder Creek still fills me with wonderment… and gives me the chills.

The Devil's Chains

Date posted: March 1999

This story involves my paternal grandfather. I don't know if it's true, but it is a good story.

My great-grandmother would always tell my grandfather that if he ever misbehaved or disrespected her, the Devil would come with a chain and drag him down to Hell.

Well, one night he stayed out a little late night, drank a little with the boys, and by the time he decided it was time to head home, it was well after midnight! Needless to say, he was scared to start with. Not only was it well past the time he was to be home, but he was also drunk. He knew his mother would be very upset with him.

Knowing that he couldn't stand at the doorway of his friend's house all night, he set out down the road to his house. It was a dark night, with no moon in the sky. He could only see the unpaved road because it was lighter than the grass around it. All the while as he walked, he kept thinking about what his mother had said.

"If you misbehave or disrespect me, the Devil will come with a chain and drag you down to Hell!"

Needless to say, he was getting more and more scared. He came to a point in the road where he had to pass between two fenced cow fields, and on over a hill. Just past that was his home. Right about then, he heard it, the unmistakable sound of dragging chains, right behind him.

His heart leaped out of his chest. There was someone—or something—only a few feet behind him, and they had a chain. He just knew it was the Devil, coming to drag him to Hell.

He started to run, not daring to look back into the face of the Devil. Behind him, he heard a low moan, obviously the Devil calling out to him. And worse yet, he heard the sound of hooves on the road as the Devil ran after him. All the while, the sound of that jangling chain echoed in his ears.

He ran even faster, but the Devil was closing in. He heard the low, mournful moaning sounds only a few feet away, and that chain. He crested the hill, thankful for the pull of gravity as he sped up going down the other side.

In the distance, he saw the lights of his house and someone standing on the porch. It was his mother! She was screaming… no. His mind reeled. She wasn't screaming. She was… laughing?

Yes, standing on the porch steps, laughing at him as the Devil got ever closer.

He ran into her arms, crying and begging for forgiveness that he misbehaved and disrespected her, begging her to pray to make the Devil go away.

But she just laughed at him, and the poor old cow with the chain around its neck that had gotten lost… and followed a familiar face back to the barn.

Door Ghost

Date received: October 1998

I had a whirlwind romance that led to a very bad marriage. I married Eric when I was 22. He was in the Navy in Norfolk, Virginia, and I decided to move down there to join him.

Not knowing the city at all, I was drawn to a particular old building in Norfolk's Ghent area called the Aberdeen, on Redgate Avenue. The building still had the dumbwaiters to bring coal up to your apartment and the original coal sheds in the basement where past tenants could store their own personal supply of coal.

We rented a three bedroom apartment on the first floor. It had wood floors, a claw foot bathtub, and steam radiator heat. I was in heaven. We used one bedroom, converted the second into the TV room/library, and the third room, because it had no radiator, served as storage and a possible guest bedroom with a day bed.

Our marriage, which lasted only six months, began going sour as soon as I moved down to Virginia. I soon discovered that I had company in the apartment. The "company" resided in the bedroom that we had reserved as storage. I always had a feeling that I was being watched, but I was never scared. This something looked out for me. It turns out it hated my husband.

I would always try to keep this door to the bedroom closed. I would close it, listen for the click of the door, and check the door by pushing against it. I would walk two steps down the hall and hear the creak of the door open. After repeating this several times, I decided to let it remain open. My cat used to have a ball playing with something in that room. The stranger part of this is that whenever my husband closed the door, it stayed that way.

Once he was taking some laundry downstairs to the basement, which was creepy enough by itself, and left the back door open for a few seconds. He closed the screen door, which had to be forcefully closed as it scraped against the concrete. Our kitchen was directly above the washing and drying machines and he definitely would have heard someone enter the apartment.

When he came back upstairs, the screen door was locked. This was a metal hook lock that had to be swung into an eye or metal loop. My husband had to climb through a window to get back in and proceeded to search the entire house as he thought someone had broken in. Nothing. It locked him out on several more occasions.

When I moved out, I maintained contact with some neighbors in that building. When we would go out, I would always sense something watching longingly from the window of that bedroom when we walked by.

Frank's House

Date received: October 1998

I have another story on your site, called Door Ghost.

When I left Virginia, I had managed to find the love of my life after the worst marriage of my life. I joked that I had to get married, to move to Virginia, to get divorced, to meet my soulmate.

After spending two years in Virginia, we decided to return to my home state of Ohio. My father had bribed us with a free house. My grandmother had owned the house when she died and my uncle had died in that same house shortly after. The house had been a rental for about fifteen years and was the eye sore of the block. The deal was renovate it and it was ours.

It was a big task and we actually thought twice about it. The house was dark and creepy, almost as if it were unhappy. The house was built in 1928 and you could tell someone at one time had really loved this house and had put a lot of work into it. It had fallen into disrepair since then and the house was visibly sad looking.

It all began one summer evening at dusk. I had been left alone in the house for the first time and I was scraping linoleum glue off of the kitchen floor. I heard thumping in the basement right under where I was sitting. The thumping then began to run the length of the house, as if someone was in the basement pounding on the ceiling. Although I was freaked, I continued to work. And sing. I sing professionally in musical theater productions. My singing seemed to calm the noise, especially older songs from the 30s and 40s. Even to this day, when I play Glenn Miller, an exuberant peace pervades the entire house.

The noises continued and the presence in the basement was so thick. You would be working on something down there—rinsing out paint brushes, laundry—and you always felt someone over your shoulder watching, almost supervisory. Making sure you were doing a good job. My mother and I both felt it but decided to not tell my fiancé about it. One day he approached me and asked if I felt like I was being watched. I had to confess. The presence was in the basement, up the stairs from the basement, and about two steps into the kitchen. It never usually went any farther.

A pattern began to emerge—the thumping and rustling would begin around 6:00 PM every night and last until around 11:00 PM. Almost as if the person was coming home from work, retiring to the basement for an evening of work on some project, and then would go to bed. Sometimes he would even open and close the refrigerator. My dog would stand in the middle of the kitchen and bark at nothing.

As we were cleaning up the basement, we closed the door to the fruit cellar, a little room about 4' x 10'. Big mistake. That night we heard such noise from that basement, like something was trapped and fighting to get out. We never closed that door again. To this day it is still propped open.

We began to get a little fed up, especially when you came up from the basement with laundry and something chased you up the stairs. You could audibly hear the swish-swish of trousers rubbing together and footsteps behind you. He had called my name once and even went so far as to goose me one day when I was vacuuming.

We eventually went downstairs and had a little conference. We told him he was welcome to stay but this was our house and we really loved it and were doing our best to fix it. We didn't want to see him or hear him anymore because he was frightening us. All was pretty much quiet. However, the day it all ended was when we had glass block windows put in the basement. The workers had removed all the old windows and the basement was aired out for the first time in years. I think he finally decided it was time to move on.

My next door neighbor, who is 72 and has lived in her house for 49 years, told me about a man named Frank who had lived there for about the same time. He had loved the house and had put a lot into it. I think he was trying to make sure that we took care of his "baby."

Howling Dogs

Date posted: November 1997

My apologies if this is a repost. I didn't see it out there in the newsgroup, so I assumed it had been eaten by the ether. I thought I would relate a Samhain story... 'tis the season, after all.

It was around a week before Halloween when my friends Jerry, Brian, Neil, and I all decided to play a sort of macho version of tag. I'll explain. It was a game of our own making. Basically, it consisted of us going out into a wooded area after dark, one person gets designated as "it," and everyone else scatters like mad and hides, just like we all remember. The macho bit comes about in how we get "tagged." "It" has with him a crossbow, and bolts with, instead of points, padded bags about the size of a silver dollar.

Well, it being about a week before Halloween, we decided to go out and play our version of tag out at Mount Lebanon, an area known for occult activity (mostly rumor and legend, but a few strange things have occurred there). We were careful not to go within the boundaries of the actual Mount Lebanon property line because there's a Christian retreat up there as part of the property, of all things, so we ended up in a wooded area east of the place.

We parked Brian's Monte Carlo by a big incinerator, and headed out into the woods, with Brian as "it"; he just enjoyed shooting us, I think. We were scattered all over the woods, all of us with that tingly "someone is hunting me" feeling pumping up the adrenaline, all of us waiting to hear a twig snap or the twang of a bowstring, waiting to feel the whap of one of those damn bolts popping us or hear it whack a tree. The only way to keep from getting shot was to become "it." You could only do this by getting all the way to "it" and tagging him before he can shoot you. So, generally, you heard the crossbow string pop and dashed like mad to try and tag him before he reloaded.

Well as I said, I was out in the woods, waiting, when I heard a tick-tick-tick, fwoosh sound, which sounded for all the world like a gas stove lighting up... a *big* gas stove. I started thinking about the incinerator and figured it must be on a timer... at least, I *wanted* it to be on a timer.

The "someone is hunting me" feeling was no longer much fun. "Someone other than Brian is watching me" started taking over and I began thinking that risking a bolt in the chest might be worth it. If I stepped out of the woods, he would shoot me for sure, but if I stayed in the woods, the non-Brian whoever ("that lit that incinerator," my brain kept yammering at me) might do more than that.

Then I heard Brian saying that maybe we should leave in sort of a higher trying-not-to-sound-scared voice from near the car. I came out of the woods about the same time that Neil did and we headed for the car. The incinerator *is* on, and, because it had a padlocked switch, we believed Brian that he didn't switch it on. The padlock was gone and the panel was wide open, but we managed to convince each other that someone who worked out there must have snuck past a hyped-up and armed Brian, gone up there, silently unlocked the lock, opened up the panel and switched it on, then snuck back down the open road... sounded reasonable to us! All this time, Jerry was missing. Then we heard the howling.

Jerry came bolting out of the woods at a dead run screaming at us to get in the damn car NOW. We didn't question him. We started diving in, me into the back seat with Neil, Brian flipping madly through his key ring and already in the driver's seat.

Jerry was about twenty yards or so from the car when we heard the screaming from the tree line. We all looked behind Jerry, and coming out of the tree line was a young girl, obviously terrified, and the howling had degraded into snarling and barking. Close behind her were several large black dogs resembling Rottweilers, all of them in full pursuit and all of them had their teeth bared in apparent fury.

Jerry dove into the car and immediately tried to slam the door shut, but Neil brought up his foot and stopped the door from closing, kicking the door halfway open in the process. The girl was screaming at us to please help her, Jerry was screaming, "Trust me, let me shut the damned door," Brian was whimpering as he tried to stab his steering column to death with the ignition key, and I was frozen in the back seat, staring at the dogs and this little girl through the heat haze coming out of the front of the incinerator.

Jerry managed to whack Neil in the shin and slam the door shut as the little girl slammed into the side of the car, screaming and begging us to let her in. I remember her sounding so scared, her blonde hair all around her face, obscuring her features.

The dogs kept coming at a full run and I was sure that I was about to watch them tear her apart like puppies with a stuffed animal, when the dogs stopped. The little girl stopped pounding on the side of the car immediately, and calmly stepped back as the dogs all sat down at the same time, like they were at a dog show or something. I remember most of all the very adult smile that crept across her face as she locked eyes with Jerry, like a woman playing coyly with a prospective lover. It was a sickening thing to witness cross the face of a child, or at least a child-like thing.

I have no idea what would have happened if we had kept that door open, or what would have happened if Brian hadn't at that moment managed to start that big damn canary yellow car and torn down that road. I whirled around in my seat and watched as the girl and dogs were enveloped by all of the dust being thrown from under the tires of Bruce's car.

Happy Halloween...

Eight Toes

Date received: November 1997

Okay, as I've said before, my family on my mother's side were moonshiners. They lived in a long dark hollow called Duncan Fork in West Virginia. Theirs was a large family. It consisted of my great grandfather, his wife, and if I'm not mistaken, either 12 or 14 of their offspring along with the wives and husbands of the ones that were married. All or most of them lived in Duncan Fork and raised corn and sold moonshine to support their families. The time was around the late 1920s and/or early 1930s. My grandmother said that most of the women would work the fields and watch for the law, but there were always some of them on guard with rifles.

She said it started with one of my great uncles seeing something while returning from making a delivery of shine. The deliveries were always made after dark. While coming back across the mountain between Bias, West Virginia and Duncan Fork he heard a loud scream, like something dying or in great pain. When he stopped his wagon to see what it was, he saw a large dark animal of some kind on the opposite side of the hill from him. He said it was not a bear or anything he had ever seen before. When it started to come across the little hollow towards him, he shot at it with his rifle, but it didn't seem to have any effect. It just screamed and ran away.

After this it was seen many times in the following two years or so around Duncan Fork. It was shot at many times, but with no apparent effect. They started calling it "Eight Toes" because when its tracks were found, they always had eight toes. I can't remember if there were eight on each foot or only on one.

My grandmother told me about one time when my grandfather was bringing a load of sugar across the hill, and the thing suddenly jumped into the trail and swung a paw or arm at him. It missed him and he took off as fast as his horse could go. When he got home that night, there were four deep cuts across his horse's side and a 50 pound bag of sugar had been torn open. Grandpa said he'd shot at it with his pistol, but didn't know if he'd hit it or not, the way his horse was jumping around.

Grandma told him that the thing had been sent to punish them for the things they were doing. She said there had been three lawmen killed on Duncan Fork the day the thing jumped Grandpa.

There were many accounts of the thing getting after the men and tearing up their stills while they were either making moonshine or bring stuff in to make it. But she said it never seemed to bother the women.

One time she and another woman were going to draw water from the well late at night when it stood up behind the well housing. She said it was at least seven to eight feet tall and stood and walked away on two legs like a man. She said it was hard to tell what color it was, but she thought it was a dark brown.

About two years after the thing was first seen, the law finally did get in to smash the stills in the head of the hollow, after killings on both sides. The thing was not seen after this. Maybe it was something sent by "whoever" to help stop all the things going on at the time in Duncan Fork, who knows.

Doll at Dawn

Date posted: August 1994

My cousins, two of them, lived about a half hour away from my old house. We would visit them frequently when we were small. My cousins, two girls, shared a room and they had a bunk bed. One night when my brother and I slept over their house, something occurred that I don't have any explanation for up to today. My brother slept with my youngest cousin while I shared the top bunk with my other cousin. We were kids, and the bunks were big enough to hold two small kids comfortably.

Suddenly, I woke up. My eyes just opened, none of this stretching and slowly coming awake crap. It was early morning, between the time where night ends and dawn begins, when the light is bluish. Pale bluish light filling the room, you know what I mean? Well, I sat up in bed in the top bunk. The room had that eerie look, due to the blue light and the perspective from the top bunk. At the foot of the bunk beds, there was a dresser with a huge mirror on it. There were few things on this dresser, little girl things, dolls, jewelry boxes, and so on.

I was fully awake, and knew it. I looked over at my cousin at my side, she was sleeping. I looked outside the window, which was at my other side of the bed. It was starting to get lighter. Then, I looked at the dresser. On the dresser, in the center, there was a huge doll, one of those old fashioned kinds, with full, ugly pastel colored dress, bonnet on its head, glass eyes that opened when it was upright and closed when you laid it down, those type of dolls. This doll was looking right at me.

I didn't notice anything unusual until it started to move slowly. It moved its head and looked out the door into the hallway, and blinked its eyes. Then, it slowly turned its head back towards me. I sat there, in terror. I started to tremble. I was so scared. I didn't know what to do. The doll blinked at me again. I was suddenly filled with horror. I can't explain it—I was so uncontrollably terrified. I wanted to scream, but couldn't. I kept staring at this doll. It moved its arms up a bit; it was those type that was jointed, like a Barbie doll's arms. It repeated the process of turning its head towards the door and back to me.

While staring at the doll, I reached over and tried to shake my cousin awake. She wouldn't wake up (she is a deep sleeper). I don't really remember what I did next; horror probably blocked out some of it. The next thing I remember, I was in my Aunt's bedroom, screaming for her to wake up. She woke up, and asked me what was wrong. My screaming had woken up the kids, and they came into her bedroom. I told them what happened.

All of us walked back to the kids' bedroom. I was so scared to point out the doll, but I managed to do so. My aunt went over to the doll, and checked it out, and stated that I must have been dreaming. The only person that believes me is my cousin that I was sharing the bunk with. She told me that a few things happened in that house, such as hearing steps pound up the stairs, and nobody appearing.

From that day, I would never, never go into my cousins' bedroom by myself. Thank God they have moved, and we moved, so I don't have to worry about that anymore.

Missouri House

Date received: March 1998

I lived in an older two story home on a hill in an older section of Maryland Heights, Missouri. The house was divided in half to allow for two separate living areas. These two areas were connected by a walkway which also led to the basement/wash room and afforded another bedroom towards the rear of the basement. My great foster grandparents always lived on one side of the house and at various times, five of their generations occupied the other half of the house. A younger uncle had occupied the basement bedroom.

What I know is that my foster Great Grandparents (who were very religious) were always aware of strange "goings on" but chose not to go into detail other than to reaffirm those of us that thought we were losing out minds. They lost many a piece of china when the cabinet doors would fly open and the china would fly out both in front of them and at times when they were in other rooms. The cross that hung above their bed was frequently turned upside down.

All of us at one time or another clearly heard our name called from the basement, but upon checking it out no one was there. The "voice" always seemed familiar to us and therefore we were certain it was another family member. Items would disappear from one side of the house and reappear on the other, but not immediately—it would often be about the time you gave up hope of ever locating it.

On one evening, my foster sister and I, who shared one side of the house well beyond the puberty years, and were night people, had just finished cleaning the kitchen spotless. Within minutes after leaving the kitchen to watch some television in the next room, I returned to the kitchen for a drink, only to find a cross necklace, which had been lost weeks earlier on the other side of the house, lying right in the middle of the perfectly empty, clean kitchen table.

There was an "atmosphere" to the house that was absolutely depressing and yet it was difficult to talk yourself into leaving. My sister and I made a vow not to leave the other alone, especially at night. Lights would flash, music would be turned off and on via a radio, and if we were playing records the needle would often be "pushed" across the album. In the upstairs, a rocking chair could often be heard rocking, yet there was no chair up there. Bees somehow got into the upstairs en masse but fairly quickly died.

On nights when I was unfortunately left alone, I would often see a black figure coming from the kitchen, through the living room, and into one of the bedrooms. Because the bedrooms did not have doors but rather drapes hung, I would also see the drapes move as if a breeze blew through. Other things happened that I have only spoken of to my husband because they were so horrible that I find it nearly impossible to believe, and yet had to tell someone or go insane.

As I said, every one that spent time there was aware of events that could not be explained by logical, normal circumstances. These people were of varying ages and beliefs. Some would acknowledge but not go into detail, as if discussing it would cause something worse. Some of us were trying to find the answers and some would quite simply avoid the subject. When I tried to get the family to search for help and the history of the house or land, they vehemently opposed the idea for fear that we may cause harm.

I lived in the house for an entire year, working nights in order to avoid what I felt was the hardest part of the day to deal with this, before I totally lost my cool and screamed out my resentment at what was going on. As soon as I finished my tirade, the water pipes blew right where I was standing. Shortly thereafter I married a man just so I could get out of this house. Needless to say, the marriage did not last, but that seemed a piece of cake to handle in comparison. I have since moved out of the state and have no idea if the house stands. Whatever it was, it was pure evil.

Double Doppelganger

Date posted: September 1997

About two years ago, my cousin and I got into a conversation about the supernatural. We talked about Ouija, reincarnation, and ghosts and stuff, until he decided to tell me something he experienced a long time ago.

It's a bit difficult where to start, since they're actually two separate experiences, but they do tie together. I'll just tell them in chronological order, as he told me.

Around '62, when my cousin was about four years old, he was sitting somewhere in the middle of the living room of the house his parents and he lived in at that time. He remembers in quite a bit of detail what was going on at that moment.

They had visitors, and his parents let him play with his toys while they had a conversation. He remembers he was very sad about something, when suddenly his attention was drawn to an upper corner of the room. He looked up, and saw a spirit "floating" up there, which was watching him.

He failed to recognize it, although it seemed very familiar. The spirit had a rather sad expression on its face. Then suddenly, he recognized the face as being his own, only twenty years older. He just knew he was watching himself, my cousin explained, although he couldn't have any idea how he would like by then. He just sensed it.

He kept staring at the older "spirit" of himself, and after a few seconds, the face showed some kind of recognition, and smiled at him. After a friendly nod, it disappeared. His parents were still conversing.

About twenty years later, he came home from work and was pretty tired. If I recall correctly, he had some troubles with his girlfriend at the time, and had no interest in watching TV, so he planned to go to bed early.

He sat down on the sofa and suddenly he felt a presence, as if he weren't alone in the room. His attention was drawn to a corner of the room, where he saw a little kid playing with some toys. He remembers staring at it, while blinking his eyes to make sure he was awake, but the kid really was there.

Again, he didn't immediately recognize the little child, but the kid didn't seem afraid at all, and even showed recognition on its face. A few seconds later he realized what was going on... he was looking at himself when he was a kid! Over the years, he had forgotten his initial experience, nor did he really understand what happened back then, but in a fraction of a second he recalled this experience he had as a kid. He felt a bit sorry about the kid/himself being sad, and tried to comfort it with a friendly nod. The kid smiled back at him and vanished.

I'm the only one he has ever told this story too, and although I have never heard anything like this again, it really fascinates me. I know there's a name for experiences similar to this (people seeing their own ghost) but I never recall a story of people seeing themselves at different ages.

Any comments on what this could be, what could have caused it, or even similar experiences?

Best Friend

Date received: May 1996

Hello all, have I got a doozy for you.

Four years ago, my best friend was killed in a hit and run accident here in New York. I was shattered, as one could imagine. It happened during a Memorial Day cruise around New York. She had been afraid of boats for all of her life, and just that once decided to board a ship, where she had gotten extremely drunk. I tried to convince to her to come to a club with me, but she wanted to go on the cruise. I did my best to change her mind, but she was dead set on going on the cruise. And she went, had a great time, and when she left the ship, and was about to cross the west side highway, she dropped her glasses in the street, bent down to pick them up, and this car came out of nowhere and hit her head on. It dragged her four blocks and that was it. Luckily (or so they say) she was killed instantly.

I attended her wake five days later, and said my final goodbyes, but I couldn't attend her funeral. I was unable to help it—I would have had a nervous breakdown. I'd known her since kindergarten. During the time since her death, I'd been unable to sleep for more than an hour or two each night, I was that wracked with guilt.

However, two days after her wake, I was lying in my bed crying, like I had been for several days since her death, and sleep was nowhere to be found. While I was waiting for my body to give in and fall asleep, I felt the distinct presence of someone, followed by pressure on my bed. I looked over my shoulder, saw the impression of a (large, and that she had) rear end at the end of the bed. I said out loud, "Oh, that's just Diane." With my words, the impression left the bed, and I was able to fall asleep. I've slept well from then on.

For years now, I've been trying to convince myself that it didn't happen, but deep down inside, I know it did. It was her way of telling me to let go and get on with my life. And she's still here—I can feel her every now and then, helping me out. Hey you, stop laughing, I'm telling the truth!

In closing, yes, I do believe.

Dragging Chains

Date posted: November 1994

This experience happened around 1975.

My brother Carl and I lived at home with my parents while we were working and going to college, but every summer my folks would take off, just traveling around the U.S. and leaving us to house sit and mow lawns. One particular warm humid night not long after my parents left, I came home from work, watched TV, and went up to bed. My brother was already asleep in his room, which was next to mine.

As I lay down in bed, I heard the distinct sounds of a medium to heavy weight link chain being dragged on the other side of my bedroom ceiling directly over my bed. It sounded exactly like a person picking up a length of chain, dragging it across a flat surface (there were no floorboards in this attic space), and then dropping the chain to the floor again. It would then repeat itself, yet the noise never got any distance from the spot overhead. I listened to this eerie sound for three nights in a row, each time reasoning with myself that there had to be a rational explanation for it. I kept it to myself, least my brother think I was crazy. It bothered me that he never indicated that he heard anything at all during the night and I was becoming worried that I was the only one who could hear this.

On the fourth night my nerves started to frazzle. That night shortly after I went to bed the sounds started up but, instead of directly overhead in the attic, the sounds of the "pick up, drag and drop" of the chains changed location, and were now on the other side of my bedroom wall. The very wall my bed was pushed up against. Accompanying the noise of the chains was a thumping sound against the same wall. I had an unshakable feeling that there was an intelligence behind it and that I was the target of the cacophony, as if the noises were intentionally directed at me. I was beginning to wonder if I was going a little nuts myself.

The following morning before we took off to attend to our differing schedules, I asked Carl if he ever heard noises in the attic at night that he couldn't account for. He replied that he hadn't.

I began to tell him about the "pick up, drag, drop" of the chains but he cut me off by tossing a dirty look. He thought I was putting him on. That night I heard the chains start up not long after I climbed under the blankets. I was not surprised that the sound of clinking chains had resumed their original position back overhead my bed. I shut out the noise by placing pillows over my ears.

The following morning, I came downstairs and noticed my brother looking tired. With much trepidation, I cautiously asked if he heard the sounds that I had told him about the day before. He looked at me with wide eyes. "Yes, I heard it," he replied. It was very clear he'd been shaken up and didn't want to discuss it. Disappointed by his attitude, I was still greatly relieved to know I wasn't hearing things. All I really needed was the confirmation.

Other strange things happened in that house that I won't go into, but as for the sounds of the chains, they went from a nightly occurrence to being present only occasionally. After about eight weeks they disappeared altogether. It was only then I checked out the empty attic. There was nothing up there that could account for the constant eerie clinking of metal one long ago summer.

I have posted this letter in a few places asking if anyone has ever had the experience of hearing ghostly chains. So far no one has replied to this question. I ask, because the phenomena itself (chains rattling or dragging) seems peculiarly confined to fictional stories, for example, Charles Dickens' "A Christmas Carol." Yet what I heard was most definitely the sound of dragging chains!

So I ask: Is there anyone out there that has this experience with chains? I am very much interested if you have.

Also, has anyone any idea what the sound of chains could mean? I welcome any comments at all, even negative ones at this point. Looking for answers.

Icy Touch

Date received: July 1997

Wow, what a response! I guess I'll share another one with my adoring fans (joke). This is yet again another story told to me by my stepfather. It's a little creepy, so hold onto your computer mouse for comfort.

About twenty years ago, my stepfather and two of his friends were renting an old house in Liverpool, Nova Scotia, Canada. It was rather remote, I guess, and the locals had tagged it as being "haunted." The men scoffed at such notions, and moved right in, forgetting all the silly warnings.

A month went by no with no real problems. Everything seemed calm and serene. One night, however, my stepfather and one of his friends decided to stay up late, light a fire in the fireplace, and sip some cold ones. They assumed the fire was out after dumping soot on it, so they went to bed.

At 3:00 AM, my step-father felt something cold, almost icy, on his shoulder. He bolted awake and he could smell something smoldering. What could it be, he asked himself. Oh no! It must be the fireplace! He raced downstairs and got there just a split second before a big log was just about to roll onto the floor, flames shooting every which way. He ran over and flipped the log back into the fireplace with a pair of tongs.

Yet another two months went by without any other happenings. One of the guys had the bright idea of using an iron to iron their clothes for work the next morning. Well, they did not unplug the iron, and the wiring malfunctioned and blew a fuse. My stepfather was again woken up to the touch of icy fingers on his shoulder, and was able to fix the problem without much difficulty.

Two weeks later, he was shuffling through some old things in the ancient attic when he found a diary. It seems that fifty years before, there had been a girl living in the house who had kept a diary when she was about 14. She had watched her drunken father drive over a nearby cliff with his horse and buggy one night, and she went hysterical. Her mother, a cold, unloving creature, decided her daughter was insane, and locked her up in the attic, only giving her bread and water once a day.

My stepfather turned the diary in to the local museum, where they told him the girl had eventually died in her room, where the attic was now. It didn't take long for these three grown men to pack their bags and leave!

Blood Stain

Date posted: July 1995

Well, I've had no fewer than eight requests for more, so here's a good one. This is about a haunted duplex.

Across the street from the fairgrounds is a row of older housing authority duplexes. They are all somewhat run down, and the population in the area consists mainly of recently unemployed or unemployable persons. One of these units, on the east side of the second building from the corner, had been re-rented sixteen times in the space of two years, often by people who moved away to identical units in the same row. A friend of mine was hired to clean this unit and redo the kitchen floor, so he brought along his usual staff of three people in addition to himself to do this.

When they arrived, things seemed normal enough. All of the surrounding units were empty and waiting to be refurbished in the same manner as this particular one, so it was very quiet. The bathroom upstairs needed some serious help, so my friend went upstairs with the other two men to see to it, while the woman they had brought along to help worked in the kitchen.

While washing the floor, she moved aside the stove and under it was a bloodstain. It looked as fresh and new as if it had just been spilled. She tried to scrub it off, but every time she succeeded, she'd turn her back while the water was drying and it would reappear. After three times doing this, she started to get freaked out and called the men to come down. They all agreed that it was strange, so they ripped up the linoleum.

This solved the problem... for about 20 minutes. Blood started to ooze from the floorboards, looking half-congealed. She couldn't believe it. She yelled for the men to come down again, and they did. They agreed to go home and try again the next day, saying it was probably a dead or dying cat or dog.

The next day, they returned. The bloodstain was on the floorboards, so they decided to re-cover the floor. This took the morning, but when they were done, the floor, one solid piece of linoleum, looked as shiny and new as a show home. Satisfied, they returned to cleaning the upstairs.

After about fifteen minutes, the woman in the kitchen dared to look at the floor again. It was back, but that wasn't all. That section of the linoleum had somehow reverted to the dingy, gray, dirt-encrusted look of the previous lino. She dropped the bucket she was holding and tried to scrub it clean. Of course, it didn't work. But, as she was scrubbing, the sobbing and screams of a young boy made themselves heard.

The men upstairs heard them too, and came rushing down the stairs. They found the woman fainted on the kitchen floor, so one of them stayed with her while the others went to find the source of the cries. The sound didn't exist outside, or in the adjoining or surrounding duplexes. Only in that one. They quickly gathered their gear together and left. My friend dropped off his workers at their homes, then went to talk to the people at the housing authority.

It turned out that that unit, which had been built in 1936, had been occupied during the 60s by a young single mother and her eight year old son. They lived relatively quietly until the boy's father came by one day to see him. The father had an argument with the mother, and a struggle ensued. In the melee, the father's gun went off, killing the boy. Both parents ran, not wanting to be charged with murder or manslaughter, leaving the boy to bleed to death alone on the kitchen floor. The linoleum has been changed in the duplex twelve times since that happened, but the blood always comes back. None of the tenants who have lived there since have stayed longer than a month, some of them preferring to live on the street.

Well, there's the end. My friend only went back once, just to see. The last renovations included two layers of lino. It hasn't helped.

Colombia House

Date received: November 1998

Story note: I'm not very much of a writer, but if you bear with me I hope you can get a good story.

This happened in 1985. I was 24 at the time. I live in Bogota, Colombia. I had a girlfriend who lived with her mother in an old house. They lived far from my own home, so many times when it got late I'd stay over.

There are two basically two things that happened to me in that house that really got me wondering about the supernatural. The first was one night I was sleeping in a very small room right down the hall from where my girlfriend was sleeping. About 1:00 AM the door was pushed open, hitting my feet that were close to it. I woke up and heard running towards the end of the hall. I thought it was my girlfriend playing a joke on me so I got up quickly to catch her, but instead of seeing anyone I found nothing. I went to her room and found her fast asleep. I woke her and told her what had happened but she didn't believe me.

Afterwards, nothing strange happened until some months later. In the city there was power shortage and every night from 8:00 to 10:00 PM there were blackouts. My girlfriend's mother had to go out of town for a month, and since my girlfriend studied I was volunteered into babysitting her younger brother and watching the house to avoid burglary. I arrived at the house every night a 6:00 PM, and at 8:00 PM the lights would go out because of the blackout. Every day when I arrived the little brother would stick to me like glue. I would watch TV until the lights went, and then with candle light read something.

Nothing much happened during the first week, then one night in a room next to the living room I started to hear footsteps. Since the floor was wood, you could clearly hear the creaks. I immediately got a flashlight and went into the room thinking someone had broken in, but the room was empty. When I got to the middle of the room, while I was pointing the flashlight in front of me there came a creak from behind me. When I turned around to see what it was there came another creak from behind, making me turn around again.

This happened to me about five times when I decided that wasn't for me, so I headed out of there, closing the door behind me. When I got out, the little brother was there scared as hell telling me that he always heard the same noises from that same room. I decided to stay out of there for the rest of the night, but I still kept on hearing the creaks. That happened every other night I was there, but I didn’t go in the room again.

After the babysitting job, I tried not to stay there very much, but from what I was told by the little brother the noises kept up practically every night.

To keep the story short, I never could discover what was going on, but not long after a police detective came one day to the house, making inquiries about a woman who had died in that house of childbirth (unrelated to my girlfriend). When he showed us a layout of the scene, the body was located precisely in the room where I had heard the noises. I don't know if that's the problem or not but to me it could be.

Crawling Girl

Date posted: September 1995

Here is an interesting story that was related to me by a friend. I preface this by saying I do not vouch for its authenticity, but must also say that my friend was quite sincere and compelling when he told me this little gem.

One evening around the fall of '81, my friend was driving home from work. It had been a long, tiring day, and as he put it, "All I wanted in the world was a hot meal, a cold beer, and a soft bed."

Before he could reach his offramp, he ran into a really bad auto accident. Traffic was being diverted, and he was forced to take an exit he'd never had occasion to take before.

After a few minutes of driving, he realized that he didn't have a clue where he was. At that time, he was a newcomer to the town, and a little shaky in his navigating. He kept his eyes peeled for any sort of road marker which would take him back to the highway so he could try to backtrack, but saw nothing.

It was only a little after 7:00 PM, but already the sky had darkened quite a bit since leaving work. He kicked on his headlights and saw a mom and pop sort of convenience store ahead. It was dark and obviously closed for the night, but he thought he may find a pay phone so he could call one of his buddies from work, who could get him on the right track.

He pulled into the dirt parking lot, and, leaving the motor running and lights on, climbed out of the car.

While walking toward the store, he told me that suddenly he got this really odd feeling, like something was out of sync, but what, he couldn't say. He stopped and looked around the woods surrounding the store, the hairs on the back of his neck tingling.

He saw something at the edge of the tree line, and after a minute made out the figure of a woman apparently crawling from the woods. Well, immediately he figured she must be hurt or lost or something, and he ran over to her. By the time he reached her, she had collapsed onto her back, and just lay there.

He said she seemed to be in her early twenties or so, plump, but not fat, with long dark hair. As he kneeled beside her, she glanced at him, and he said something in his stomach seemed to give a slow tumble. Her skin was very pale, but streaked with mud. He said it was as if she'd taken a mud bath or something. He asked her the usual, "Are you all right? What's happened?" and etc. She never spoke a word, and he decided she must be in shock or something. He touched her forehead, and said it was ice cold. He was in a flurry, wondering what the hell to do. He wasn't even sure where he was, and had no idea how to help until he remembered that he'd stopped looking for a phone in the first place.

He told me that he took off his jacket and draped it over her, then ran back to the store. Unfortunately, there was no phone at all, and furthermore, it seemed obvious that the place had been closed for years. He was just about to bundle the girl up in his car and just drive until he found anything at all, when he saw some car headlights.

He rushed out into the road and flagged down the car. There were some kids inside, young high school football player types, as he described them. He explained what had happened, and lead them back to where he'd left the girl.

Well, of course she was not there. Even his jacket was gone. There was no evidence of anyone having been there at all: not a leaf crushed, not a speck of mud, nada.

My friend figured she must have pulled herself back into the woods, and so with a little pleading, he got the kids to help him search. He turned his car toward the woods, and got the teenagers to do the same. My friend searched until he began to worry about running out of gas in his car, and as he backtracked, following the light, he saw the teenager's headlights swing back toward the road. He ran to the parking lot, but couldn't reach them before they bugged out on him.

Well, what the hell do you do? My friend stood there, deciding which option to follow, when he said, again, he got that funny feeling. He turned around, and by God, there was the girl again, crawling from the edge of the woods. My friend said he felt his hair literally stand on end, because there was no way she could have been in those woods and not been found. Not in the shape she was in. As he stood there, petrified, he saw her collapse on her back again. She lay there for a few minutes (my friend said he just couldn't move a muscle), then begin to choke and grunt, as though she couldn't get any air. Then suddenly, my friend said she was gone.

Well, that seemed to break the paralysis, because he said he ran for the car, smacked into it, fell down, jumped up, and somehow fumbled the door open. He said when he turned the car around, as the headlights washed over the woods, he again caught a glimpse of something pale crawling from among the trees. That, as he said, was too much, and he peeled out of there like a bat out of hell.

Eventually he found his way home, and here, really, the story ended. He told me that for the first few weeks after that, he had really bad nightmares about the incident, and also, until he told me last year, had never related the story to anyone.

What it was all about, he never knew, and I think never bothered to find out. He never told me what town it took place in, though I pushed him pretty hard on that. My friend thought I was a sick puppy for being so interested. I explained that I only wanted to maybe verify the story, but that was a mistake, because he got mad at me for doubting him.

I have a theory, and for those of you who've stuck it out this far, I'll share it with you. Maybe someone has a better one, or, and this is what I really hope, my theory might be close enough to the mark to strike a chord in someone.

I believe that the girl worked at the mom and pop store. One night she was robbed and shot, or stabbed or something, but not killed right away. The person who robbed the store, believing her dead, dragged her out to the woods and buried her in a makeshift grave. Sadly, the girl possibly regained enough consciousness to drag her way from the ground and back to the store, where she finally did die of her injuries.

Furthermore, I believe the person who did rob the store was a local person, and the killing was an accident. A stranger would have most likely left her where she lay, but a local person, maybe fearing discovery, might possibly try to hide the crime.

At any rate, that's the story. As I said, I won't vouch for its truthfulness, because I don't have any facts to back it up. I suppose that is the nature of the ghost story though, and why so many doubt that they could exist because cold, hard facts are so hard to come by.

I apologize for the length. This being my first post, I should have probably trimmed it down a little. But if you want more, I've got more, because I am interested in these strange asides. Unfortunately, I myself have never had an experience even remotely approaching the ghostly or supernatural. I sure envy those of you who have. All I can do is listen and pass along.

Elderly Woman

Date received: May 1996

My server is in the middle of a merger and a move and our news server is down so I can't access the newsgroup. But I wanted to share this with you.

When my daughter was born four years ago, I was living in a house in which an elderly woman had lived just prior to us. She lived alone with nothing but a cat for a companion. One day she had a massive heart attack in the kitchen and died on the kitchen floor. It was four days before she was found by a police officer, who broke into her house in response to a call from a neighbor who hadn't seen her for several days. Her cat was lying curled up next to her.

We had several clues that she was still present in the house. For instance, when the kitchen light was off our cocker spaniel puppy would stand at the kitchen doorway with his hackles up and bark like crazy, but we never saw her until the day I brought my baby home for the first time. I had a c-section and was having a hard time getting in and out of bed. At about 2:00 AM on her first night home I woke up to her crying and needing to be fed. Her crib was in my room at the foot of my bed.

I rolled over to struggle out of bed and saw a human figure by the doorway to my bedroom just inside the room. There was a little bit of light coming in from a street light outside and, at first, I thought it was my oldest daughter checking on the baby. But I thought it was peculiar because she was wearing a big floppy hat, like a fishing or gardening hat. I called out her name and she didn't answer. I called out again and this time my daughter came into the room. When she flipped on the light the figure disappeared.

The next night, I again woke up in the middle of the night to my baby wanting to nurse. I noticed the figure again but this time it was sitting kind of squatted down by the door, as though it were trying not to be noticed. I panicked and yelled for my daughter. Again when she flipped on the light, the figure disappeared.

Talking to the neighbor across the street a few days later I found out that this lady was an avid gardener (I could tell that from all of the flowers in our yard) and always wore a big floppy gardening hat. She also loved children and especially adored babies. I think she was excited that there was a newborn in her house and just wanted to help me watch over her a little bit. This is an honest to god true story and it's not the only time I've seen a ghost. Let me know if you want to hear another one.

Edna's Ghost

Date posted: October 1995

Greetings. I just got into newsgroups recently and have thoroughly enjoyed reading about the ghostly experiences of others. I also have an experience to share. My husband and I have kept this experience pretty quiet for fear of upsetting neighbors. This is due to the fact that we believe we lived with the ghost of a woman who was well-known with many living relatives in our tiny community.

When my husband and I married six years ago, we lived in the home he had purchased from the family of "Edna" (name change to protect the family). Edna had been living in a nursing home for a few years and would not be returning to her home. Edna and her husband had built this house in the 1930s. She used to babysit my husband and his brother when they were children. After we had been married for about a year, we received word that Edna had died. The following events began a week after her death.

It began with my husband. Several times while crossing the road to the mailbox, he heard a woman call his name. He would return to the house and ask me why I called him, which I hadn't. Then the radio in our kitchen "malfunctioned"—it began playing continuously even though it was turned off. We finally unplugged it and packed it away. After disposing of the radio, the television began acting up. First it would turn itself off. We assumed it was overheating. But then it started changing channels by itself, just random channels, in addition to turning itself off.

I started calling surrounding neighbors to see if anyone had recently installed any new remote control devices such as garage door opener, satellite dish or whatever—no one had. After weeks of this, the TV started coming on by itself in the middle of the night and we'd have to get out of bed and turn it off. Sometimes it would come back on as soon as we had gotten back into bed. We took it to a repair shop three different times and it always functioned just fine there, but would always malfunction as soon as we brought it back home.

We own an antique eight-day wind-up clock that has never worked. Several times it chimed. It wasn't wound, and there were no vibrations in the house or any other causes we could find. The pendulum would begin swinging, the clock would chime seven or eight times, then the pendulum would stop.

Finally, one day while sitting at the kitchen table talking and having coffee with my husband, a dark but transparent "form" came from the dining room, walked behind my husband, and disappeared. My eyes must have been huge because my husband immediately began asking me what was wrong. The form resembled a shadow—it had the shape of a person but no features. This happened again to me and twice to my husband; we would trade places at the table in hopes that we would see it.

One morning at around 2:00 AM I got up to go to the bathroom. The bathroom had a door from the bedroom and also another door connecting to the kitchen. I had a strange feeling that I needed to go into the kitchen so I opened the connecting door to the dark kitchen. This time I saw a form but it was like a glowing white mist. I had turned off the bathroom light so it was pitch black around me. It came towards me and I actually jumped out of its way and let it pass! I was terrified but didn't feel threatened.

A few nights later, I woke to the sound of jewelry moving around in my antique jewelry box. I woke my husband, turned on the light and the sound stopped. The jewelry in the box seemed untouched.

Another instance involved a coffee cup that my son had given my husband (his stepfather) as a gift. The cup said "you are loved so very much because you are so very loving." It had been badly chipped but my husband didn't want to discard it for sentimental reasons. So we stored it behind some antique dishes on the top shelf of an old china cabinet in the dining room. One morning when I got up and went to the kitchen to fix coffee, that cup was sitting in the sink. I checked the china cabinet—the other dishes were undisturbed and unmoved. My husband and son swear they didn't get it out (my son couldn't have reached it anyway).

We have since moved to a new home. I must say we never felt threatened by this presence, although it was scary. My husband and I have often talked about how, when one of us would be alone in the house, we never really felt "alone." They day we moved, I stood in the middle of the house and invited "Edna" to come with us. When I later told my husband what I had done, he laughed and told me he had also invited her to join us. She didn't, however. We love our new home but it certainly lacks the feeling of presence the old home had.

Foot Slapper

Date received: January 1999

I have had many paranormal experiences in my life, but this one was one of the most frightening.

My husband, son, and I were living in an apartment in Costa Mesa, California. Soon after moving in I began experiencing something or someone hitting my foot as I lay in my bed. I always sleep with my foot or feet out of the covers in order to cool down.

As I lay in bed, in the dark, something would slap my foot, very hard. I could hear the impact also. It felt as if I were being slapped by something cool and flat. The feeling was like being hit on the bottom of my foot with a child's toy sand shovel. The impact was even hard enough to send my foot flying up over the over foot.

Terrified, I would jump up and turn on the lights, looking for whatever could have done this. I also checked my son's room for intruders or ghosts or whatever the heck I could find that could explain this strange phenomenon. Of course, I never could see anything or anybody there at all besides our own family. My son was sound asleep.

I didn't wake my husband, as he always acted as if I were slightly crazy if I mentioned any of my experiences, a really frustrating way to live, I might add. I probably had this experience three or four times in this apartment before we moved to a condo in the same neighborhood.

That's when things really picked up in the paranormal department. My son began experiencing strange shadows and voices in his room, and I felt very cold spots and extremely negative and dark vibes all over the condominium, especially in the entryway and the bedrooms. I was also experiencing a vile smell once in a while and began getting really ill. My husband, of course, never smelled the strange odor.

My son began sleeping in our bedroom out of fear of his own room. I would put him to bed, read him a story and pray that the bad vibes that I felt in his room were really nothing. But, I was constantly scanning the room as I read to him, as it always felt like something was moving, just out of sight. The room always felt heavy with a dark emotion tied to it somehow, as did my own room. I would wake up and find Dan sleeping on the floor of my bedroom, right next to me with just a pillow and blanket. My son was only seven years old then.

One evening, while reading in bed, a strange bright blue light began pulsing from my thumb as I held the book. I can only assume that I was seeing my own aura, but why? It stopped as quickly as it had started. This phenomenon repeated itself a few days later.

Then one night as I was reading, my husband asleep next to me, something hit my foot again very hard. I sat up, petrified, and said out loud, "Go away, leave me alone! You are not welcome here." The ceiling in my bedroom began to pop. It was a high vaulted wood ceiling. The popping became louder and faster. Then, I saw a shadow go by outside my bedroom window. It was at the top of the window and looked like fabric floating or sailing by, very quickly. The popping and shaking of the wooden ceiling became very loud. Then suddenly a white smoke appeared at the foot of my bed in front of me. It took the shape of a long "V." It stayed at the bottom of my bed for a moment and then quickly shot up through the ceiling and was gone.

The popping and shaking stopped immediately. The whole thing was over just like that and all that remained was dead silence.

The next morning I called a psychic center in Anaheim and they agreed to come to the complex and do a clearing for me. After the clearing, the condo did feel better, but I didn't like it anymore. My marriage was breaking up and my son and I moved out shortly after the clearing. I have never experienced the foot slapping since. I have had many psychic experiences and would love to share some of them you all if you are interested.

Chilly Elgar

Date posted: May 1995

I made the acquaintance of a ghost while living in a student dorm in a less fashionable area of Kensington. It was a three story house with a communal kitchen on the second floor, a bath on each floor, and three largish "bedsitter" rooms with old coal fireplaces converted to gas heaters on each level. I was on the third floor, and when I walked down the stairs to the kitchen I would feel someone walk past me going up. The first time I was surprised but didn't say anything to my housemates. After a few meetings I just decided to ignore it. I got so used to it I just automatically stepped to the side to let it pass. Always the same feeling of light pressure and a cool breeze. The house was across the street from the London residence of the composer Edward Elgar, so I began to call the ghost Elgar in honor of its former neighbor.

The bathtub on the third level was under a sloping roof. I'm very tall so it bugged me, as well as the fact that most student housing in London didn't have anything resembling a shower, and if they did it was never hot and the tubs were all built for pygmies. If I slid down to avoid hitting my head I had to bring my knees up halfway to my chest. Washing my long hair was such a pain I chopped it off halfway through my stay.

One late night trying to get clean, I heard heavy footsteps on the stairs. I knew it wasn't one of my mates on the third floor; they were all female Chinese students and had light steps. I was surprised that one of the boys from the first floor would be coming up, and a little alarmed as I was having a bit of a conflict with one student. The damned door had no lock and if anyone wanted to be nasty they could. Of course, I was homesick and one of my symptoms of homesickness was paranoia (the other was a craving for Mexican food, unheard of in London at that time). I was hoping for a long warm bath, since no one else seemed to be in and I would have what little hot water there was all to myself.

Anyway, I was kneeling in the tub, rinsing the shampoo out of my hair under the spigot and turning off the water when it got cold, usually after running lukewarm for thirty seconds, when I heard these footsteps. I straightened up, whacked my head, and turned to get my towel figuring I was about to be barged in on by a belligerent student who also wanted hot water. The steps paused outside the bathroom door. Then, nothing.

So, I froze, figuratively as well as literally, water dripping in my eyes. I had goosebumps and the willies thinking some crazy British serial killer was outside my bathroom. Well, I figured he was hoping to nail one of my tiny Chinese roomies and that he wouldn't be prepared to fight a big strong American girl who fenced and played field hockey.

I decided to get out of the tub as quietly as possible. The door was behind me to my left. I kept my eye on the mirror above the sink opposite the door for any signs someone would enter. The single bulb above the mirror started to fade out. I thought at first it was about to go out, and of course was mentally cursing a blue streak when I noticed what appeared to be an ice halo around it—you know, like on a very cold, clear night when you see rings around the moon? And the dark was closing in on the light. The bulb burned steadily, but it seemed to grow less and less bright.

"Elgar, you creepy SOB!" I yelled. "This isn't funny, you snotty English bastard, and I'm not impressed, so get the hell out of my bath and leave the hot water behind!" I was of course frightened half out of my mind, but figured with the other half that if it was a serial killer he might think Elgar was a roommate and leave.

Nothing. The room stayed dark as I struggled to pull jeans on over wet skin. I got a sweatshirt on and reached to open the bathroom door. The handle was so cold it hurt my hand.

I opened the door and saw nothing. The hall was perfectly normal. Nothing there, no one there. I ran into my room and turned on the gas in the fireplace. I felt like ice. I couldn't stop shivering for what seemed like ages. I felt like January in Chicago.

I kept meeting the more benign presence I called Elgar on the stairs, but I never took a bath while alone in the building again—I went to the YMCA where they had something resembling hot water and lots of people around.

I met a couple others but will save those for another post.

Bright Boy

Date received: July 2001

This happened two years ago, in Hilton Head, South Carolina.

My whole family goes on vacation every year. My parents and my aunt and uncle had rented a house on Hilton Head Island, South Carolina that summer for a two week vacation. My cousin David and I are best friends and usually stay together the whole time. That year, we got to share a room. The house was huge, with more rooms on the main floor then my house has on all of the floors. David and I ran through the house and picked out the coolest room in the house. The room was strange, I must admit. The far corners were made of glass, so you could see into the woods out back. I settled into my room immediately so my other cousins couldn't take the room.

David left the room to get his bags, just as I finished unpacking. It had been a long day, and it was getting dark. I lay down on the bed I chose, and before I knew what happened I was asleep. I awoke from my sleep at exactly 3:20 in the morning, because my cousin, being a chunky person, turned up the air conditioning in the room. So instead of waking him up by turning down the air, and hearing him complain all night, I decided to find somewhere else to sleep, only for the night.

I wandered the house, until I made my way outside in the back of the house. The back of the house had a deck that was in disrepair. I got many splinters in my feet from shuffling outside. The back of the house after the deck faced deep woods. However, there was a hammock on the deck that I found comfortable enough to sleep in.

I was soon torn from my sleep by a bright light in the woods. I was shocked at first, but when my eyes adjusted to the light, I saw a bright boy emerging from the woods. The boy was twenty feet away at first, but I blinked, and he was less than five feet away. He had blonde hair, blue eyes, and a huge scar running from his right ear to his lips. I was so scared that I tried to jump from my hammock, but fell out instead, scraping my face on the deck.

I woke up the next morning in my bed. I thought it was all a dream, but when I looked in the mirror I saw the scratches from the deck on my face. I never went in the back of the house again.

Dark House

Date posted: February 1995

Okay, out of lurk mode for a story.

A number of years ago, as a poor student, I was renting the top two floors of a house with seven other school chums. We thought ourselves lucky to get the house for such a low rent, plus all utilities paid for. With all of us, we each paid about $75.00 a month.

The house had its fair share of windows facing east and west, so it should be a brightly lit house in the daytime, but, somehow, the house was always rather dark and dim. We could never figure this out. Often at night, we'd hear bumps and creaks, we always put it down as the old 120-year-old Victorian-style house settling down until one night.

It was a Friday night, just around spring. Exams were done with, and winter was almost over. We were all overjoyed and happy. We felt that we did well in our exams. That evening, six of us went to the movies and had dinner. After the dinner, we headed home. The celebration continued. We were drinking pop and some of the guys were drinking beer.

We were all laughing and joking in the kitchen, when we heard the door open and footsteps coming up the stairs. We thought Jenny and Sue were home; they had opted to go to a fellowship rather than join us at our celebration. We called out to the two sisters to join us but received no answer. Tom poked his head outside the kitchen, and the dim hallway was empty.

We figured, incredible as it sounds, they probably did not hear us, so Tom went upstairs to the girls' room. A few minutes later, he came back downstairs looking very puzzled. The girls weren't home; yet, we heard someone open the front door and come up those stairs. We shrugged it off as the house settling down or a streetcar coming by shaking the house.

A week later, as I was sleeping, I woke up quite suddenly. Unsure what woke me up, I switched on the light. Looked around, peeked outside the door, nothing. I went to the kitchen to get myself a glass of water. On the way, I met another roommate who had just as suddenly woken up. We made some cups of soup and talked for about half an hour and then headed back to our respective rooms.

As I couldn't sleep, I sat in bed reading when suddenly, I heard a loud, high pitched cackle. I froze, my eyes quickly scanning my small bedroom… nothing. When I heard movement in the next room, I ran to the door and swung it open, just as Alex and Frank, the guys from the next room, were about to crash through my door. They looked rather angry as they thought I'd given that laugh. I swore that it wasn't me, when the rest of our roommates came running down the stairs from their rooms. We'd all heard that cackle.

Together we came up with a very logical explanation about what happened. We figured that the tenants renting the basement and first floor of the house were partying and the sound carried through the vents to our rooms. Sounds reasonable, right? The next day, we called in on our neighbors, but no one came to their door. Puzzled, we went to the house next door where our landlord lived. Our landlady told us in a rather cold voice that the other tenants had gone home for the summer vacation and we were the only ones in the house.

Things went fine for a couple weeks. Then one night, while we were having dinner, a sudden cold air came from nowhere and the lights got dim. We stared at each other; we all looked very nervous. The already dim hallway was black as night. Suddenly, a low, very evil sounding laugh started, i's volume getting higher and higher, and that evil cackle joined it. Just as suddenly, Rich gave a loud yell.

The lights went back to the way they were before. There was no one but us in the kitchen. After that point, the conversation on the dinner table was "Why did Rich yell out?" and "How soon do we move out?" Rich swore that he felt someone grab his throat, squeezing it etc. Eventually, we decided to stay on. The rent was very cheap, and we couldn't afford anything higher. Besides, we were good friends who didn't really want to part company. Most of us were from the same town, etc.

The next day, we had to call an ambulance for Rich, who had suddenly developed a dangerously high fever overnight. At the hospital, Rich was diagnosed with throat cancer. A very strange thing as he didn't smoke and there was no history of cancer in his family. The fever was not explained; the doctors did not know what caused it as it went away soon after he was admitted. Rich was hospitalized for about two weeks. Sometime after the first three days, Rich decided that he didn't want us to visit anymore and had arranged for his things to be packed and moved to a storage facility until he got out of the hospital.

A few days after Rich had moved out, Alex and I were on dinner duty. When we heard the front door open and slam shut, we figured the others were home. We hollered out at them that dinner isn't ready yet. Our announcement was greeted with silence. Immediately, Alex and I froze and stared at each other, our eyes mirroring the horror we felt. We heard footsteps coming up the stairs. We both peeked out at the hallway… nothing. No one was coming up those stairs.

The footsteps reached the top of the stairs, and the carpet depressed as the footsteps came closer and closer. Alex yelled at the "nothing" to leave us alone, but the footsteps just continued.

We both felt a sense of foreboding, danger, as though whatever it was that was approaching us was evil.

The footsteps got to the middle of the hallway when Alex said in a hoarse whisper, "Get out of here, kid." He grabbed me very hard by my arm, shoved me away from the kitchen door, ran toward the large kitchen window, grabbed a chair, smashed the window, and practically half dragged and half threw me out the window. We were on the second floor, but we were past caring; all we knew was we had to get away from that thing. The jump gave us some bruised limbs and a couple sprains.

We looked up at the window. A shadow was at the window, then the whole kitchen slowly grew darker and darker until the window looked like a black gaping hole in the house. Suddenly, the lights came back on in the kitchen again. In spite of the fact that all we had on were T-shirts and Jeans, Alex would not let me go back into the house. It was late spring, and the temperature was still very cold but Alex made us wait on the porch until the others came home.

An hour or so later, when the other guys got home, Alex made me wait outside as they trooped into the house, got me a jacket, packed our things, called a cab, and we all headed for a motel on the lakeshore. We rented a room and stayed there for about a week until we found other accommodations.

The next day we went back to the house to talk to the landlord and pay for the window. The landlord was not thrilled with us. His wife started cursing and swearing at us. We'd told them, take the last month's rent and here's extra for the window—she called the cops on us! Luckily for us, the cops were quite understanding and polite. The landlady insisted that we did more damage than the window. We entered the house to look. What a change! The whole place smelled dank and the walls… the paint looked like someone ran something sharp over it. It really gave us the creeps.

The landlord took one look at the walls, turned pale, and refused to come into the house. His wife ranted and raved all the way through the house, though. She wanted the police to charge us with destruction of property, etc. Her husband, normally a quiet man, glared at her and told her in a rather loud voice to shut up. Surprisingly she did, for a while.

As the landlord left, with his wife yelling and nagging at him all the way into their house, the older police officer gave us a weak smile and mentioned that many years ago a man and his wife who drank rather heavily lived in the house we rented. One night, they got a call. The couple, in a drunken fit, had killed their children and the husband's mother, after which the husband killed the wife as they were fighting, stuffed the bodies into the closets, and hung himself. Apparently, the police frequently got calls from people who had lived in that house about intruders that weren't there. The police officer had grown up a few blocks away, and he mentioned that he has never known the house to be occupied by any family for more than a year at a time, or less. We were in the house for about two months.

Forest Cats

Date received: November 1997

I used to hunt a lot; I lived for hunting. This experience just about ruined hunting for me, though.

We were hunting in the foothills. I had walked up through some fairly dense woods early that morning, hoping to get a few squirrel. It turned out to be a poor hunt, so I was attempting to walk out to where my friends and I had parked the truck.

I thought it was kind of odd when a cat showed up out of nowhere. He just sort of ran up on me out of the woods. I've always liked cats, so I called him and petted him some. He was friendly enough to let me pet him, so I knew he belonged somewhere. I continued walking downhill. It seems I got somewhat confused about where I came up the hill, and as I walked I noticed I was moving sideways and off course every little while. I kept walking on, knowing that when I hit the bottom I could walk out to my friend's truck. Also, we had a special way to shoot, a signal, if there was a problem.

Suddenly, I walked out of the woods and onto a bald (a clearing on a hill side). I thought I must be a little lost, but these balds were not uncommon in the area. They usually represented where a home place had been cleared and farmed at one time. I looked around but saw no buildings. I sat down on a rock, opened my pack, and got out a can of Vienna sausages. I opened the can and fed my feline friend. He ate like he was starved.

When we were through, I stood up to get my bearings. I was surprised to see a whole lot of cats running through the grass towards me. All were meowing, the way hungry cats do just before you feed them. I decided it was time to go on down to the truck. I started walking and the cats moved along with me, meowing. They didn't harass me or get in my way, just sort of followed along. I guess there were about fifty of them. It was pretty unnerving anyway. So I picked up speed, while hoping I wasn't too lost.

At the bottom of the bald, there was an old overgrown road that led on down through the woods and I followed along it. Finally at the bottom of the ridge, I came to a wooden gate across the road. I went through the gate, expecting the cats to follow me, but they stayed inside the gate. I closed the gate. I'll tell you, I wasn't sorry that they stayed inside the gate. At that moment, the cats all turned around and ran back up the old road towards the bald. I looked back up after them, and it seemed I could see an old woman standing at the other end of the road. I could barely make out her features and it wasn't long before she seemed to walk out of sight.

I walked in the direction of the truck and presently came upon the truck and my friends. As we drove away, I told my friends about the cats. Dave, the guy driving, remarked that the cats probably belonged to the old woman who lived up on the bald. I remarked that I hadn't seen any houses up there. Dave replied, "Oh yeah, she burned up in her cabin about two winters ago. They said the chimney must have caught fire."

Sorry if this was too long.

Aunt's Books

Date posted: February 1996

I have been reading stories here for a few weeks now and even questioned if I could post here. As the answer was "yes," here I go!

When I was a teenager my Aunt Marge died. Mom was the one that found her, peacefully "asleep" with a book in bed. Mom and Aunt Marge had made a "pact" that whoever went first would find a way to let the other know if there was more to death than being dead. Well, the night after she died my aunt let us know.

Mom and I were upstairs with the cat and dog. We were comforting each other and planning the wake when we heard a huge crash downstairs. This was 11:00 PM and we were alone in the house so we fairly leapt out of our skin. We got down to the library and found that one shelf out of 20-some-odd had fallen off the wall. Now, this was in California, a mere mile from the San Andreas fault, so we shrugged, placed the shelf back on the brackets and the books back on the shelf. Mom did comment that some of the books were actually Aunt Marge's, but we didn't give it much more thought.

In the morning I got a hammer and double checked the brackets. All was secure. It was now the second day after Aunt Marge's death. Mom and I were still alone as my dad was back east on business. It was about eleven o'clock (we were to later to learn this was the approximate time of Aunt Marge's death) and you guessed it... crash! It was the same shelf. The wall brackets were still firmly in place. This time, however, the books had fallen in an odd way. Most had scattered within a few feet of the wall, as one would expect. The books that Mom had borrowed from Aunt

Marge, all of them and only them, were twenty feet away, at the end of a long passage. My Mom was very casual and merely said, "Aunt Marge always liked to make sure her point was well taken." My dad has always maintained it was an earth tremor, but Mom and I are quite sure it wasn't.

The Thing in the Woods

Date received: December 1997

This story is true and occurred in my youth. The setting is in Fairfax County, Virginia and I was 19 years old. The climax of the events took place in October of 1972. Reader beware.

My brother and I were living the typical rebellious life of the times and we had hitched back to Virginia from Ohio in August, sharing the front seat of a VW Bug as only two guys that are related could do. Upon arrival, we hooked up immediately with two characters in town known locally as the Jackal and the Rat. The Rat had just blown into town from Florida with a car that had no brakes, and the Jackal was known to have a tent.

The four of us moved into an area of woods that lay between Lee Highway and Highway 50. These woods were known to the local kids as a party place. We were located on top of a hill that had a flat area with a path that led downhill to a central crossroads of paths. One of the paths led into the deep woods after crossing a small polluted creek.

At first everything went well, and we broke camp every morning and hid our stuff in the underbrush. As time went by, we became careless and began to attract attention to our presence. We kind of felt that the woods belonged to us. Nothing out of the ordinary had happened so far.

Sometime in September we had a party and wandered through the dark woods like it was our backyard. Perhaps it was then that we attracted the attention of something else in the woods. The Rat was given to long speeches on mystical bullshit and we stayed up all night talking and smoking cigarettes. At dawn the first event occurred. As the rat was blabbing on, I looked over his shoulder and saw an enormous thing coming over the crest of the hill from the path that led to the crossroads.

Reader, I will try to describe it for you. It was three to four feet in width and it was self-contained. I say this because there wasn't any fog, but it was whitish and swirled slowly within itself. It moved its "head" as an earthworm moves its head, seeking from side to side. I had the impression that it was huge and very long, yet I couldn't see a tail as it was down the hill and my view was at the crest. I shouted for the Rat to look and it vanished. I ran the twenty feet to the spot and looked downhill and saw nothing. No sound, no sensation, no fear, just wonder. We should have left then but we were young and foolish.

Our camp was discovered by the police and we moved deeper into the woods, down the hill, across the creek, and about fifteen feet off of the path in a low area that was hard to spot coming from the crossroads, but gave us a clear view of the path coming from the deep woods. Our life continued as before and we roamed the woods, mainly in search of easy firewood and a way to escape if the police came back.

The first thing that I noticed was a sound during the day as if someone was throwing rocks through the tree canopy. I could hear the tearing sound of them passing overhead but none ever came down. Strange but not worrisome. Then we began to hear noises at night. Something walking around us as we sat at our campfire, distant but circling. What really disturbed us was it got closer every night.

We scoured the surrounding area for prints but found none. We realized that it was coming from the deep woods and as it got closer it made noises, low sounds, and began to break branches that cracked loudly. This bothered us as we knew there were no branches as we had picked them all up for our campfire. The

Jackal began to get scared and would scream out at it in the darkness and shine our flashlight into the woods.

The Rat, true to his nature and name, ate the last can of tuna fish so we kicked him out of our camp. He moved to a site forty feet away up on a raised area, close enough that we could hear him playing his harmonica but out of our sight. One night he came screaming down to our tent begging to come in. He was shouting that "Beelzebub" was chasing him. I awoke and was giving him hell and asking if he was drunk. Then something that gives me the chills to this day screamed out and the Rat dove thru the tent flaps right into my lap.

I turned to my brother and tried to wake him up. The screaming continued like nothing I have ever heard, like a wounded animal crazed with pain, rabid. I kept shaking my brother to wake him and couldn't believe that he was still asleep! Then I heard the running of heavy footsteps, two feet running. Now I was scared. I literally shook my brother off the ground and was yelling with the Jackal and the Rat in fear. It came right up to the tent screaming. Then, thank God, it returned to the deep woods running and screaming until it grew fainter, but it never stopped screaming.

I questioned the Rat about how this thing had begun to chase him. He said that he was asleep in his bag when he heard something walking up to him in the dark. I asked if he saw anything, but he said that he only saw something dark looming over him grunting, and when it screamed he jumped up and it chased him. He was sure that it was the Devil.

People began to know that weird things were going on with us in the woods, but we toned it down as they also thought we were strange. Many scoffed, but when they came for a visit they asked for an escort back up to the road. Once at the crossroads, when you turned right to enter the deeper woods to our camp, a black curtain was waiting. You could not see your hand in front of your face. It was here that "Beelzebub" would wait for us. As we would enter the Jackal would bend over in fear and whimper. My brother and I would take off our belts and be ready to lash at anything that would lunge at us. We heartlessly would kick the whimpering Jackal before us in the vain hope that the thing would leap on him first and we could get away. The thing would walk on our right side and stay with us until we would reach camp.

We began to notice that as each month passed it would begin to circle the camp, coming closer each night, breaking limbs and making low sounds. As I stated in the first story, my brother expressed disbelief about such a thing being out in the woods. He slept most of the evenings and he had a midnight shift job at Jack in the Box. One night that thing was very close and the Jackal and I kept hearing it around us. My brother got up to go to work and I told him not to go through the woods tonight but to go the long way. He refused, but did ask for a broom and the flashlight to knock the spider webs out of the path.

The path was about a mile and a half to get to the highway. My brother went into the deep woods and I stood on the edge of the camp listening… it was moving after him! I waited for the horrible screams but heard none. In the morning my brother woke me by pulling my foot and telling me that he believed. Oh yes, he now believed. He said that he didn't hear anything coming up behind him, but suddenly the bushes next to him exploded in a frenzy of motion with loud grunting sounds coming out of them. My unbelieving brother dropped the broom and the flashlight and ran all the way out of the woods, down the highway till he got to work.

So much for September, reader. October was on us and it was getting really cold in our little tent. We used a candle to warm it at night and built large fires to keep the night and cold away. I only had two wool army blankets, one under and one over. I got up a lot to stoke the fire at night. One night, three of us were sitting around the fire and I was facing the path that led into the deep woods. From it I saw two approaching figures. Two adult males, the taller in the front, single file wearing white robes. My first thought and words were, "Look at that, now we've got the Klan."

However, the two men didn't seem to notice us, and they were walking in a strange fashion. Both had their arms tight against their sides, bent at the elbow, stiff in front like they were carrying a book. But there wasn't any book. They drew near, almost opposite of us, then they did seem to see us. They turned towards us and began to bend over as if to see us better or to bow, then vanished from the feet up.

I had electric chills yet had to know. I jumped up and ran the fifteen feet to the spot on the path. No sound, no sight of them. Neither one of those guys were flesh tone; they were as white as there robes. We agreed among ourselves not to speak of the event as no one would believe us and our local reps would only sink lower.

We had two girls that used to bring us food sometimes and they had promised us a peach cobbler one afternoon. They never showed, so we went looking for them on the path by the crossroads. About fifteen feet from the crossroads we found the cobbler and dish upside down on the ground. Alarmed by this, we fanned out and searched for them in the woods and down the highway at a local hangout. They were there and began to babble upon seeing us. They stated they would never return to the woods again under any circumstance. They said that as they approached the crossroads, they saw four men sitting in a circle, wearing white robes. One was wearing a "funny" hat.

Now in those days it wasn't uncommon to come upon people hiding out smoking weed or even wearing funny hats. As the girls got within fifteen feet, they saw that something was being passed around the circle and then all four vanished. We could only look at the girls, as we had not told anyone about the two we had seen recently at night. We now realized that it was for real.

Reader, you may ask why did we hang around? Well, we just didn't have any other place to go, but we would be forced to find some place as events unfolded and the weather got a lot colder.

I had a dream that the figures in white were using the screaming thing that walked on two feet to get us to leave the woods. We wanted to but we just felt there were few options. The police were aware of us and had begun to stop us often and tell us to move on or jail was going to be in our future. That ruined our chances for sleeping in abandoned cars.

We had worked for a company passing out flyers for a dollar an hour to get our beans. They were moving out of their old building to another town and we helped them pack. The building was close to the woods on Lee Highway just across from King David Cemetery. This building had been many things: an inn, a restaurant, and the business we worked for. Upstairs was three apartments and on the wall some wag had written, "Davy Crockett slept here."

In our desperation to get away from the woods and all that they held, we kicked in the back door of the vacant business and went upstairs to the three apartments. We laid down our stuff right at the top of the landing in the first apartment. There were three windows that looked out onto the gravel horseshoe-shaped drive and on across the highway at the cemetery.

We went to sleep and I was awoken by a loud crash that vibrated the floor beneath me. It was well-lit in the room by streetlights outside. I looked to see if my brother was awake or the Jackal heard the sounds, but they were asleep. I thought that it was another bum looking for some place to sleep and had kicked in the door as we had done. However, I heard someone walking on gravel below us. Now, that couldn't be possible as we had swept up the floor before the business left and there wasn't any gravel. The only gravel was out in the driveway.

I got up and went to the window to look out, but no one was there and I could hear them downstairs. Then the footsteps started up the stairs. I pulled my blankets up to my chin and was sitting up and facing the stairs. When the walking stopped there was no one there. My mind just couldn't accept more supernatural stuff so I told myself that I must be dreaming. The whole thing happened again, starting with the crash waking me from my sleep.

In the morning I told the others about what happened and we moved further down the street to a Sunoco gas station that had some old cars parked around it. God bless the owner. He didn't call the law even after he discovered our presence. He watched over and tolerated our being there on his lot. Eventually, I got a job there running the midnight shift and we got a car for ourselves. My brother and the Jackal could sleep in peace and they would drive the car around in the day while I slept in the back.

The Rat was always hanging around our little world but he was on the outs with us due to his nature. He came up one night to the station begging me to let him stay in one of the cars. His straw hair was all over the place and his hand was slashed in the palm. I asked him what was wrong and he began to tell me that he had kicked in the back door of our old job site and he had gone upstairs to sleep in the first apartment. (We hadn't told him what had happened to us there) He related the same chain of events to me, but he said that when the footsteps stopped at the top of the stairs he saw a tall white shape that moved towards him. He had broken the second story window when he jumped out and cut his hand. He had left all his stuff, including an expensive camera. He begged me to go there with him in the day. I did but I saw nothing. There was a room with open rafters past the first apartment and it had a terrible feel and chill to it. We didn't stay for long.

That's about it, dear reader. I really haven't had any more experiences since, and I have been in some dark and terrible places in my travels to twenty-seven countries. What was it all about? I don't know. If you don't believe that's ok by me. If you have some time and you wish to go there and see for yourself that's ok too. I haven't been back. I last saw the Rat and Jackal in gas stations working or just hanging out.

If you wish to comment about/question I will answer.

Window Man

Date posted: April 1995

I have a really frightening story that happened a while back, and I have never told many people, only because it brings back bad memories. When I was five years old, we were visiting family in New York. The adults were in the living room and all of us kids went into the kitchen to play cards. There were about seven or eight of us seated at the very long table. I was at the head of the table, facing the window, and one of my cousins was at the other head with her back to the window.

About half of an hour into the game, I looked across the table. To my horror, there was a large figure standing outside the window looking in at us. The figure had no discernible features. It was a silhouette of what appeared to be a human form, like a shadow. It was wearing a hat that looked like a fedora. What frightened me the most was that this thing made sudden movements, then peered into the window, and gestured like it was trying to get into the kitchen through the window.

I quickly jumped out of my chair and pointed toward the window. I was paralyzed with fear and could not speak. The other kids looked, and they all saw it as well. We ran out of that kitchen screaming. My cousin, who had her back to the window, turned around and ran on top of, and across, the table in order to get away from this Shadow Man lurking right behind her.

Upon hearing our screams, the adults quickly ran to us, but the figure was gone. When we told the adults what had just happened, they did not believe it was possible. You see, the kitchen window was on the second floor of this large house, and it would not have been possible for anyone to be standing outside the window. True story.

Has anyone out there had an experience similar to this one?

Old Farmhouse

Date posted: March 1999

I live in rural Virginia, and my high school, believe it or not, was in between two pastures in a very agrarian area. Although I was never much into sports, I had a few friends who were, and several were on the cross country running team.

The course laid out for the cross country track took a meandering path around the school, then out into the pastures around the school, with the permission of the farmers, of course. One part of the course took the runners past an immense old farmhouse, abandoned and dilapidated on the crest of a hill overlooking the school. There were, of course, rumors that it was haunted, but to my knowledge no one ever saw or heard anything there. It was just a big, old, spooky, abandoned house.

At times, the cross country runners did see someone poking around there, but it was obviously the owner of the property as they would see his truck parked in front of the place, and they could see that he was using the downstairs rooms to store equipment and surplus hay.

That being said, I shall relate the story of my friend on the cross country run, and the subsequent discovery made by myself and some intrepid companions one day.

Her name was Jessie, and she was on the cross country team. She was hardly the star member, and would, unfortunately, often find herself running alone. That never dampened her spirits, however, and she remained on the team doing her part. One day, when as usual the pack had left her far behind, she found herself alone as she trudged up the hill towards the old house. Glancing up, she saw someone walk past an upstairs window. She thought nothing of it, of course, assuming it was the farmer. It didn't dawn on her until later that his truck was not in its usual place in front of the house.

She told this to her circle of friends, and some of us decided to check the place out the following day, which was, fortunately, a Saturday. So, we met in the field at noon and tromped off to explore. What we found there was the typical old falling-apart farmhouse. Empty rooms, except for the equipment and such, creaky floor boards, and piles of wet shattered plaster, beer bottles, graffiti, and cigarette butts. Then we rounded the corner from the old living room to go upstairs, and each of us stopped dead in our tracks.

There were no stairs. Apparently, the stairwell had collapsed into the cellar long ago, leaving only a yawning opening ten feet above a tangled pile of old timbers on the cellar floor below. And yet, Jessie had sworn she had seen someone walk by an upstairs window. We explored the house more completely, now being very careful since we knew just how bad off the place really was. We didn't find any second staircase, and there was no way to reach the second floor. It's a mystery that has remained unsolved, as in the middle of our exploration we heard the truck door slam outside, and we all beat a hasty retreat out the back so we wouldn't get caught trespassing.

I don't know if it was a ghost she saw, or if it was someone who could climb like an orangutan, but it's all a moot point now. That house was demolished only one year later, and a nice shiny new modern split level was erected in its place. I wonder if the owners of that house have any late night visitors.

Hunting Lodge

Date received: October 1998

The year was 1981. I had just graduated from grammar school. On that same day we received a phone call that Uncle Hank had died. We went to the wake, which was in the Catskill Mountains in New York, in June.

That August my family and I went back to the Catskills for summer holidays. My father has a hunting lodge there with his brothers. Therefore, we would spend two weeks happily away from the city. Nothing happened the first week and all went as usual.

On the second Friday, it all changed. I was awoken at 4:45 in the morning by a sound. My parents and I had our own room at the lodge on the ground floor by the kitchen. My folks where on the big bed and I was across the room on a bunkbed. The noises were coming from right above us on the second floor. Heavy footsteps, drawers opening and closing.

Now, the house we were in was very secluded, with no one for about ten miles all around. I thought perhaps we had a burglar. I listened as the steps went down the stairs to the living room. There I heard the ashtrays being moved about and the strong smell of pipe tobacco began to fill the air. Then the footsteps went through the dining room to the kitchen. At this point I was scared to death. The footsteps reached outside the door. The air seemed to change and I screamed.

My dad jumped up and ran over to me. He then went to the door and opened it. Then it all stopped as if someone shut off a large machine. My mom woke up and demanded to know what was going on. My father took me into the living room and tried to calm me. He told Mom that we might have a burglar and told her to stay with me. He got a shotgun and searched the house but come up with nothing. All the doors were locked as were the windows.

I said that it must be the ghost of Uncle Hank. My Father said it could not be as ghost they don't come out at 5:00 in the morning. Later that day when I was alone with Dad he told me some shocking news. First, the noises started at 1:00 that morning and that when he got up a few times to check it out there was no one there. Second, right after Uncle Hank died, his brother Jim was in the house alone and heard someone calling to him but could never find the person.

Over the years the hunting lodge has had a lot of ghostly things happen. People who come up for hunting season have seen and heard a lot of strange things. One morning one of the hunting wives saw a man on the sofa smoking a pipe. When she asked her husband about the man, he was confused. There was no one of that description in the lodge. My father showed the lady a picture of himself with Uncle Jim and Uncle Hank. She pointed out Uncle Hank, and she left that day. My brother has heard the footsteps and door slamming as well. The ghost is still active and every hunting season someone sees or hears something.

Apartment Handprints

Date posted: June 1998

It was the last place we would have expected to have trouble with. Our first apartment was in one of the standard large complexes that you see popping up in suburbia. It was about twenty years old, but here were a lot of old fruit trees on the grounds, so it may have been built on the site of an old farm stead, something that is common for our area. Maybe our difficulties stemmed from this. On the other hand, such complexes tend to have a high tenant turnover and some residents can leave suddenly.

Anyways, it started out with the usual irregularities that often accompany these incidents. Lights would be on or off when you would swear they hadn't been that way when you left the room. The same goes for doors opening and closing. Objects would be moved from where you had put them and pictures would go all askance.

At about the same time when it began to dawn on us that there might be something to these occurrences, the fingerprints started. Again, we didn't realize at first what was happening. It just seemed like my husband and I were getting extremely messy. I was constantly wiping dirty fingerprints and handprints off the walls.

At first it was in places that you would expect, around light switches, for example. Then it got stranger. Fingerprints and even whole handprints began to appear way up near the ceiling, which couldn't be reached unless one was on a ladder. Toward the end, some even appeared *on* the ceiling. I pulled the desk out to retrieve a fallen piece of paper and found the wall behind it just plastered with handprints. The prints were too small to be my husband's or mine. We guessed they were the size of a child's, or now, in retrospect, the size of a small woman's hands.

One night I wiped the prints off the hall light switch, and then carried some dirty laundry to the hamper in the bedroom. I didn't touch the switch, yet when I came back, the prints were back. I wiped them off, turned, walked away a couple of feet, and turned back. The prints were back. I repeated this six times before I gave up, and just left the prints. By this time our walls were just in a constant state of being peppered with prints, to the point that company would stare a little.

My husband and I watched one afternoon as the bedroom door unlatched itself (we heard the click), swung open, and then swung shut again.

One evening I walked into the bedroom to find a living bedspread composed of bees crawling around on our antique redwood bed. All the windows and doors had been shut. When I returned with the manager, they were all gone except for a few stragglers.

The moving objects became more brazen towards the end. We would hear a loud thump in the other room, or right behind us, and find that something quite heavy had fallen. Books would seem to have just flown right off the shelf. Things turned up in increasingly bizarre locations. One evening, I went to retrieve the broom from the hall closet. It wasn't hanging in its usual spot. Now, while there is a possibility that I used it and forgot to hang it back up, I know I didn't leave it where I eventually found it: standing in the bathroom, precariously balanced, bristles down, atop the sink faucet. I reached to take it down, and it fell to the floor the moment my fingers grazed it.

Here's the grand finale. When I was quite pregnant with our first son, I got up in the middle of the night to go to the bathroom (big surprise). When I returned, I was in the narrow space between the wall and my side of the bed when I happened to glance down at the floor. I was standing in a spectral woman that was lying on the floor. She was very small and thin-boned, elderly, and was writhing around as if in great pain. The expression on her face was ghastly.

I let out a shriek that was in itself bloodcurdling, and jumped onto the bed, clear across my side and onto my husbands, crushing him under me and nine months of baby. To this day, many moves later, I can't sleep on that side of any bed, and I still leap in and out of bed, because even though it didn't "get" me that time, there's always next time.

Stepfather's Goodbye

Date received: December 1998

My stepfather Paul and I were very close even though he had seven biological daughters of his own. He was 65 years old and lived in Florida with my mother. His health had been failing due to heart bypass surgery recently and he passed away building a fire in his fireplace. My mother was home that day in the other room attending to something else and found him in front of the fireplace and he was gone. There was nothing the paramedics could do to save him.

Paul and my mother are originally from the state of Ohio, as am I. The funeral would be here in Ohio so my mother flew Paul's body up here for the services. She stayed with us in our little ranch house that Paul helped fix up from time to time while he was alive. He did a lot of remodeling in my bathroom, such as all the plumbing, flooring, and painting while I was at work. He was very generous in that way, always helping his family in any way he could without expecting anything in return.

I think I should explain to you how my bathroom is set up so you'll have a better understanding of what I experienced the day after Paul's funeral service. My bathroom is "L" shaped with the main entrance door of the room directly from the long hallway that adjoins the bedrooms also. There is a door at the end of the "L" that leads directly into my bedroom. So, there are two doors to this room, the hallway door and my bedroom door.

Mom was sleeping in the spare bedroom directly across from the bathroom hall door. The day after the funeral, I woke up at 3:30 in the morning having to use the bathroom. I always keep the bathroom door shut that leads to my bedroom. When I get up at night, I never turn on any lights as I just walk directly to the bathroom door, open it, and flip on the light directly next to the door opening. When I got up that night, I walked to the bathroom door and opened it. There directly standing in the bathroom/bedroom doorway stood a dark figure that was large. I could not make out who it was because I had not turned on the light yet. It looked like a black shadow of a large man, and Paul was a big man.

My first thought was one of my teenage sons were up wanting to come into my room for some reason. I spoke out loud and said "Justin, what are you doing here standing in front of my door for?" Right after I said that, I turned on the bathroom light and there was nobody standing there at all. I looked down to the other door by the hallway and it was shut. Nobody could have left the bathroom that fast and shut the door too without me hearing and knowing it.

I know it was Paul stopping by to say goodbye to me. He did so much work in that room and I feel it was his way of telling me he was okay. My husband and I had told him when he was sick to not be afraid of dying and that he would be okay. He tried to believe us, but I know he was afraid of dying. This was Paul's way of telling me everything would be alright.

I have never seen anything like I did that night since his death. I know he went on to his wonderful second life. Nor have I ever experienced anything like this in my life before. I never even thought about ghosts much or spirits, but what a great thing Paul did by stopping by to say his last goodbyes to me. He told my mother one time that I was once of his favorite people in his life and I truly believe I was.

Fish House

Date posted: March 1999

I was 16 or 17 years old and worked as a shrimper out of Beaufort, North Carolina. I was trained as mate by the owner of the boat, Captain F, who was 72 years old and lacked the strength and stamina of his younger years. Finally, I was given command of this 25 foot channel net boat.

The boat was moored at an old fish house on Taylor's Creek that was literally built in one day by the boat owner's father, "Captain P," in the 1930s. I had strange feelings while working in the old fish house quite often, but never felt anything malevolent. Other sounds were heard, but I always attributed the sounds to nets and other equipment settling in the loft and other places (this place was stuffed). Captain P when alive had a reputation for being a hard and even abusive individual. He supposedly tolerated few people and was particularly hard on his boys, two of whom I knew well.

One night I was shrimping in the river when a huge storm started approaching from the west. Quickly, I retrieved the net into the towed skiff, and headed for the fish house just as the storm hit. The storm was as bad as I had assumed it would be and I could only move at a slow pace. The seas in the river rose up to about four feet and the rain came down in torrents, but I eventually reached the relative safety of Taylor's Creek. The rain and wind subsided before I reached the fish house, but the lightning was still illuminating the skies as the storm passed to the east. During a few of the lightning flashes, I saw a face looking out of the window wearing a pair of glasses. The face was definitely a male face and he had a thoughtful look on his face.

As I approached the dock, I saw Captain F standing on the dock frantically pacing back and forth. He helped to tie the boat, inquired to my safety, and then went on board to make sure that the boat was ok. As I walked through the door to the fish house, I saw Captain F's wife sitting on the old couch that was inside. She was very calm and was smiling cheerfully. I asked her what she found amusing and she said she was laughing at her husband being in such a tizzy over my safety. She then stated that she knew I was ok because Captain P told her so. I asked if Captain P wore glasses and she went on to describe the wire rimmed glasses I had seen during my approach. She added that Captain P had been standing by the window, amused at his son's antics on the dock.

Captain F's wife did not get along with Captain P when he was alive, but she told me that since his death, they got along quite well. He had been drawn to her, as she was very sensitive and no one else in the immediate family could see him. She later told me that she only saw him in the fish house, usually when Captain F was worrying about something.

There was one other time Captain F's wife had a psychic experience that I witnessed, but I will save this one for another time.

Attic Collection

Date received: April 1998

This story I am about to tell you is true, and whether you wish to believe it or not is up to you.

My friend and her mother moved into a house in Frankfort, Kentucky, built sometime during the 1800s. There had been a fire there many years before, and since then it had been rebuilt. When buying the house, they were told that a father, child, and dog had in fact died in the house. Since both my friend and her mother were non-believers in paranormal activities, it didn't really make a difference.

Upon the first week that they had moved in, strange things began to happen. Rocking chairs would move back and forth by themselves without a window being opened, and the doors of the cabinets in the kitchen would open by themselves, sometimes with pots and pans flying out. On top of all this, their dog they had had for eight years died. They buried it in the backyard with all of its favorite toys.

I often went to visit my friend, wanting to be a part of the strange happenings, but nothing ever really happened until one night. They had bought a new puppy, and we all heard a squeaking noise out in the hallway. We went out to see what it was, and it was the puppy playing with a toy. But what was so strange was that that toy belonged to their dog who had died, and they had buried it with him. We all ran outside to the burial site, thinking that maybe the new puppy had dug it up, but it was undisturbed.

Things laid off for a little while for the most part. Every once in a while you could hear the giggling of a child, or see drawings in crayon on the walls. My friend's mother was no longer skeptical of what was happening; she knew that she and her daughter were being haunted. Things began missing from their rooms, such as little glass figures, sometimes dolls or stuffed animals, and no one had a clue where they had gone.

One day my friend and I went up to the attic, which no one had gone into since they had moved in. It was very dark and dusty up there, except for one side of the large room. It looked as if it had been well taken care of, and all of their missing items were lined up around the walls. Since they were not being harmed, they had decided that they would let whoever or whatever had taken them up there keep their belongings.

One night, her mother was lying in bed trying to go to sleep when a small light appeared in the corner of her room. Inside the light, there was a resemblance of a small fairy-like child, and she smiled and disappeared. My friend and her mother believed this to be their guardian angel, and that it was safe for them to continue living there without harm.

To this very day, they continue to live there, being "haunted." Their house appeared on an episode of Unsolved Mysteries to my understanding. This incident proves to me that we are really living with supernatural beings, and we should all recognize these spirits, and learn to live in comfort with them.

Web: ghosts.org
Email: stories@ghosts.org

Also by Elisabeth Busch:

The True Ghost Stories Archive: Volume 1 (2019)
The True Ghost Stories Archive: Volume 2 (2019)
The True Ghost Stories Archive: Volume 3 (2019)
The True Ghost Stories Archive: Volume 4 (2019)
The True Ghost Stories Archive: Volume 5 (2020)
The True Ghost Stories Archive: Volume 7 (2020)
The True Ghost Stories Archive: Volume 8 (2020)
The True Ghost Stories Archive: Volume 9 (2020)
The True Ghost Stories Archive: Volume 10 (2020)
The True Ghost Stories Archive: Volume 11 (2020)
The True Ghost Stories Archive: Volume 12 (2020)
The True Ghost Stories Archive: Volume 13 (2020)
Tiny but True Ghost Tales (2019)
A Survey of North American Spooklights: Eyewitness Accounts and Information on 20 Anomalous Lights (2020)
The Real Top 1000 Baby Names: Combined spellings, real meanings, current trends, & newly rising names (2018)

About the Author:

Elisabeth Busch was born and raised in New England, where there are plenty of spooks, old rickety houses, and questionable characters. She currently lives with her husband and a herd of cats in Las Vegas, Nevada, which (you may have heard) also has its share of questionable characters.

Printed in Great Britain
by Amazon

53857643R00090